WADSWORTH PHILOSOPHERS SERIES

ON

AUGUSTINE

Sharon M. Kaye
John Carroll University, Cleveland, Ohio

Paul Thomson
John Carroll University, Cleveland, Ohio

WADSWORTH
THOMSON LEARNING

Australia • Canada • Mexico • Singapore • Spain
United Kingdom • United States

For Earl and Robin

Printed in the United States of America
2 3 4 5 6 7 04 03 02 01

For permission to use material from this text, contact us:
Web: http://www.thomsonrights.com
Fax: 1-800-730-2215
Phone: 1-800-730-2214

For more information, contact:
Wadsworth/Thomson Learning, Inc.
10 Davis Drive
Belmont, CA 94002-3098
USA
http://www.wadsworth.com

ISBN: 0-534-58362-8

Contents

The biblical stories, the Gospel stories, were the original understandings, they were science and religion, they were everything, they were all anyone had. But they didn't write themselves. We have to acknowledge the storytellers' work . . .

Migod, there is no one more dangerous than the storyteller. No, I'll amend that, than the storyteller's editor. Augustine, who edits Genesis 2-4 into original sin. What a nifty little act of deconstruction . . .

—E. L. Doctorow, *City of God*

SAINCT AVGVSTIN
by André Thevet
Les vrais povrtraits et vies des hommes illustres
Paris, 1584
Courtesy of the Special Collections Library
University of Michigan

1

Introduction

When he was sixteen, the youth who would become St. Augustine of Hippo was part of a gang that stole a great quantity of pears from an orchard. They did not steal because they were hungry—in fact, they threw the pears into a pigsty. Rather, they stole simply because they wanted to do something evil.

Augustine reports this episode in his most accessible and widely read book, *Confessions*. Although he is writing about the episode from a distance of nearly thirty years, he still remembers it vividly and finds it deeply troubling. If one had to name the major philosophical preoccupation of this author of almost one hundred books, it would be his preoccupation with evil and the propensity of human beings for doing what they know to be wrong.

Augustine was not a philosopher by profession. He was a bishop, and his primary influence on Western thought lies in his role as Church Father, defining and defending the Christian faith. Nevertheless, when he was nineteen, Augustine read an exhortation to philosophy by Cicero (106-43 B.C.). It made a profound impact on him. In thinking about evil and other problems, he adopted the methods and ideas of the philosophers. His works circulated widely, starting during his own lifetime, and made a profound impact on the history of philosophy.

In this book, we aim to present Augustine's most important philosophical contributions. Unlike many thinkers who would follow him, Augustine did not take much care to distinguish philosophy from theology from autobiography. Hence, his philosophy is more easily understood against an overview of his life and work as a whole.

1.1 Augustine's Life and Times

Augustine lived the transition between the ancient and the medieval world. He was a Roman citizen living in North Africa during the final stages of the momentous decline and fall of the Roman Empire. North Africa was to the Roman Empire what the Wild, Wild West was to colonial America—it was at the outer reaches of the expansion of a very ambitious people. The difference is that, while America was able to maintain its expansion, the Roman Empire was not. Having enjoyed the culture and resources that came with colonization, North Africa was now beginning to experience the chaos and disintegration that is the mark of a government overextended beyond repair. The North Africa Augustine knew in his youth might have been merely unkempt and decadent, but by the time of his death, it was fodder for barbarian invaders.

Augustine was born in 354 into a lower middle class Roman family. He was raised in a small town located near present day Tripoli. His father was a petty bureaucrat of pagan background and his mother was a devout Christian. Although education was expensive and hard to come by, Augustine was singled out early as an exceptionally promising student. His parents arranged to send him to special schools in the hope that he would be able to secure a lucrative position. At age seventeen, he went to Carthage to learn the art of rhetoric with the goal of becoming an orator.

By all accounts, Augustine had a rollicking time in Carthage. Finding himself in the middle of a busy seaport city, away from the wary eyes of his parents, he felt anonymous and adventuresome. It is not clear what kind of drugs or music the students had in those days, but they certainly had sex. Augustine tells us in his *Confessions* that he was an especially sexually active young man. He did not let his sexual experimentation interfere with his studies, however, and he did well in school.

After a few years, he secured a job teaching rhetoric and found a steady girlfriend. He never tells us her name, though it is clear from the way he speaks of her that they were very deeply in love. They lived together, first in North Africa and then in Italy, for nearly fifteen years. They also had a child together, a boy named Adeodatus.

At this point, it looked as though Augustine was about to embark on a rather sweetly mediocre, bourgeois life. Fortunately for posterity, it did not turn out that way.

Although Augustine's father had died by now (his father had converted to Christianity shortly before his death), his mother was alive and well and could not let go of her golden boy. She followed Augustine to Italy and demanded that he break up with his girlfriend. This was not so much because she could not stand to see them living together in sin, but more because she had the expectation that, in exchange for his education, Augustine would try for a prestigious position with the Roman government. In those days, as is still the case today, the best way to land a prestigious position with the government was to travel in the right social circles. In order to enter those circles, Augustine would have to marry the daughter of someone important.

It is not surprising to find Augustine facing such tyrannical demands. The surprising part is that he gave in to them and agreed to send the love of his life away. Having secured her victory, his mother hastily arranged for his engagement to a stranger half his age. This made Augustine utterly miserable, and he had a brief affair with yet another woman to prove it.

Clearly, Augustine had romantic difficulties, which were paralleled by a rocky intellectual journey. In Carthage, he was attracted to Manicheeism, a Persian cult, and he was also attracted to the work of Sextus Empiricus (d. c. 225), which he considered superior to the scriptures read by his mother. Later, in Italy, he studied the Academic Skeptics, as well as the Neoplatonists. Augustine's inner emotional and intellectual turmoil had all the makings for a serious psychological crisis.

It was this crisis, in combination with some other health difficulties, which became the occasion of his highly celebrated conversion to Christianity in 386. Augustine was sitting in a garden contemplating his problems, when suddenly he heard angelic voices chanting "Pick it up and read it! Pick it up and read it!" He reports the incident in *Confessions*:

> Damming back the flood of my tears I arose, interpreting the incident as quite certainly a divine command to open my book of Scripture and read the passage at which I should open.... I snatched it up, opened it and in silence read the passage upon which my eyes first fell: *Not in rioting and drunkenness, not in chambering and impurities, not in contention and envy, but put ye on the Lord Jesus Christ and make not provision for the flesh in its concupiscenses.* I had no wish to read further, and no need. For in that instant, with the very ending of the sentence, it was as though a light of utter confidence shone in all my heart, and all the darkness of uncertainty vanished away. [D 146. For an explanation of

this and other bibliographical notes, consult the Bibliography at the back of this book.]

His eyes had fallen on a passage [*Romans* 13:13] in which the Apostle Paul is exhorting his listeners to give up their drunken and licentious ways. It was at this moment that Augustine decided to be baptized.

Augustine's mother is traditionally credited for precipitating this conversion, and was later beatified by the Catholic Church (St. Monica). Augustine had been building up to it for some time, however. In *Confessions* he reports attempts to curb his licentious ways, only to be overcome by weakness of will. His prayer was "God, make me celibate, but not yet."

Monica died soon after Augustine's baptism. This plunged Augustine ever deeper into his pit of despair. He gave up women, gave up the world, and returned to North Africa to pursue a quiet, monastic life with his son Adeodatus and some male friends.

But here, once again, Augustine's plans for himself were rudely interrupted. The people of the large North African city of Hippo Regius were in need of a bishop. They learned that an educated Christian was in the vicinity and demanded that he take leadership of their church. Their timing was good. Augustine was now mourning the sudden deaths of Adeodatus and his best friend, Nebridius. Accepting the invitation from Hippo was his only real option. He was ordained priest in 391 and became bishop in 396.

Although he claims not to have wanted the job, it suited him well. He became a local celebrity. He would write rousing sermons for Sunday morning. During the week, when he was not tending to his various bureaucratic duties, he found some time to contemplate and write. Given his enormous literary output, one tends to imagine him strolling or riding from one duty to another, constantly dictating to an army of scribes. The people of Hippo looked up to him and he tried to provide comfort as the Roman Empire crumbled around them. He died in 430, sick in bed, but patiently reciting psalms, as Hippo fell to a wave of barbarian invaders.

The Catholic Church beatified Augustine soon after his death. He is the patron saint of brewers, due to his self-confessed experience with loose living.

1.2 Augustine's Works

Augustine wrote a great number of works during his lifetime, all of them in Latin. His surviving corpus is larger than that of any other ancient author. These works read just as you would expect the product of a trained orator and teacher of rhetoric to read. There is no question that Augustine was an overzealous stylist, and that he thought of writing as a kind of speech making. Unfortunately, his penchant for flowery language and the clever turn of phrase often makes reading tedious, especially since the effect rarely translates into English.

Augustine's surviving works date from his conversion in 386 to his death in 430. They fall into three main categories: books, letters, and sermons. Most of the philosophical material is found in his books, though some is scattered throughout the other two categories as well. Augustine's early books are the most philosophical, both in style and in content. The later books become increasingly religious and dogmatic. It may be useful to scan the chronology of the main works we will be discussing in this book.

After his conversion in 386, Augustine decided to take what we would now call a sabbatical. He was still suffering ill health and, at any rate, wanted to devote some time to thinking and writing. Augustine retired with family members and friends for about five years. During this period, he composed a number of works, often in collaboration with the people he was staying with. Among them are *Against the Academics*, (a refutation of skepticism), *On Music* (concerning knowledge and perception), *On Free Choice of the Will* (Augustine's early theodicy), *The Catholic and Manichean Ways of Life* (ethics), and *On the Teacher* (theories of knowledge and language). Although Augustine changed his views considerably over the course of his life, he never completely repudiated any of these works, and they provided the basis for his entire philosophy.

In 396, when Augustine became bishop, he wrote a letter to a friend named Simplician. It records the shift in his thinking from the classical philosophical model to a more biblical, religious orientation. This same year, Augustine also began work on a treatise called *On Christian Teaching*, in which he further develops his ethical theory.

In 401, Augustine published his most famous work, *Confessions*. It is the first major autobiography of Western literature. In recounting the lurid details of his life, Augustine often detours into philosophy.

Barbarians sacked Rome for the first time in 410. Augustine wrote his second most famous work, *City of God*, in response to this traumatic incident. It is a set of twenty-two short books, published over a period of twelve years. In it, Augustine elaborates his political theory, contrasting the reality of the earthly city against the ideal of the heavenly city.

During roughly the same period, Augustine was working on a set of books called *On the Trinity*. The latter half of this work contains Augustine's mature philosophy of mind.

Many of Augustine's works were polemical and widely debated during his own lifetime. This was both a blessing and a curse to Augustine: he had to listen to people quoting him, misquoting him, and holding him to claims he could hardly remember making. It is not surprising, therefore, to find among his latest writings a work called *Retractations*. It gave him the opportunity to clarify and modify points found in earlier works.

1.3 Neoplatonism

Augustine did not fully discover philosophy until he was in his thirties. His education in North Africa was strictly literary. Because he failed to learn Greek, he was never able to read the great ancient philosophers Plato (427-347 B.C.) and Aristotle (384-322 B.C.). Perhaps this partially explains why he calls them "Greek pests." [A 49] Nevertheless, ever since he was a teenager, Augustine had wanted to become a philosopher. So, when his political aspirations came to naught, Augustine set about teaching himself philosophy. It was at this time that he discovered the philosophical school of thought known as Neoplatonism. Neoplatonism became a very important influence in his work—so much so that he is standardly known as a Christian Neoplatonist. In order to understand why Neoplatonism had such a profound effect on Augustine, we need to understand his religious history.

As a child, Augustine was entirely unimpressed with his mother's Catholicism. He found it simpleminded. How could an all-powerful, all-knowing, and all-loving God have made a world with so much suffering? This question, later known to philosophers as "the problem of evil," haunted Augustine, and he could not find a Catholic with a good answer.

Despite his dissatisfaction with mainstream Christianity, Augustine liked the idea of having a dramatic purpose in life. As a student in Carthage he joined a group of Christian heretics known as the Manichees. Named after its Persian founder Mani (d. c. 276), this cult claimed to offer a more sophisticated approach to religion.

Mani's great accomplishment was to present a solution to the problem of evil. Drawing on Zoroastrian myth, Mani conceived the cosmos as a giant battlefield. God and Satan are the two main forces at war. God is fighting on the side of goodness and attempting to eliminate suffering, but Satan is a formidable opponent and has yet to be beaten. Human beings are caught in the middle of the warfare, driven sometimes by the one side and sometimes by the other.

The goal of life, in Mani's view, is to identify with the forces of good and avoid any activity that could be co-opted by the forces of evil. Mani considered the crucified Christ an ideal role model: he did not give in, nor however did he fight.

Manicheism became a refuge for the café existentialists of the fourth century. The inner circle of the cult was exclusive and mysterious. They tended to be pale and thin, with exotic tattoos and piercings. They made themselves at home in university settings, they did not eat meat, and they did not have children. Augustine became a member of the outer circle—educated and austere, but not as extreme. He was a sensitive young man. Living in the rough-and-tumble of fourth-century North Africa had a way of bringing out his native angst.

Augustine gave up on the Manichees in his late-twenties after he found out that their bishop, Faustus, was a charlatan. But he never gave up on the problem of evil. For all of his life, he was keenly aware of the fragility of every kind of happiness. Augustine's two most famous books can be considered extended investigations into this issue: *Confessions* explores the battle between good and evil on the personal level; *City of God* explores it on the societal level. What Augustine personally needed in his life was an intelligent explanation of why there is so much suffering. It was only by combining the Catholic picture with his own interpretation of Neoplatonism that Augustine finally arrived at what was for him a satisfactory answer.

As the word itself implies, "Neoplatonism" refers to a set of philosophers who considered themselves followers and improvers of Plato. The key element of Plato's teachings is his distinction between the world of physical objects and the world of ideas or forms. The physical world is a world of corruption, imperfection, and change. The world of the forms is perfect, unchanging, and eternal. Because the physical world is always changing, true scientific knowledge of it is impossible. The physical world is a pale copy of the world of the forms, much as a painting is a copy of the landscape or the model. Thus, real knowledge is to be found in the contemplation of the forms, the true causes of appearances. It is this dualistic aspect of Plato's philosophy that the Neoplatonist philosophers emphasize and develop.

The most prominent leader of the Neoplatonic school of thought was an Egyptian named Plotinus (204-270). Plotinus believed that the human soul is divine. It would be perfect, were it not imprisoned in the body. The body, along with the material world in general, is an endless

7

source of evil that the soul must resist until it can separate itself and live on in its pure form.

This is the idea that set Augustine's imagination on fire. The Manichees had the right idea in absolving God of the responsibility for evil by saying that it did not come from him but rather from Satan. The problem with considering Satan the source of evil is that it excuses humans. This did not sit well with Augustine's experience of guilt and complicity in the suffering he experienced. Plotinus had the right idea in implicating the body. But he made the same mistake as the Manichees by suggesting that the body is not really part of the human person. Augustine would adapt this view to Christian purposes by insisting that humans are just as much body as they are soul. But to the extent that we freely choose changeable material goods over the changeless spiritual goods, we are responsible for the misery in which we live.

We will examine Augustine's solution to the problem of evil in detail in the following chapter. For the present, it suffices to note that once Augustine realized that Neoplatonism held within it a workable answer to the problem of evil, he became thoroughly committed to Neoplatonism.

Augustine did not confine himself to his central preoccupation. He combined Neoplatonism and Christianity in a vast array of philosophical inquiries. The main principle that launched and guided his inquiries was the neoplatonic claim that it is possible for human reason to come to know the truth about the good, or God.

One of the real delights in reading Augustine from the distance of some sixteen centuries is discovering the roots of a wide variety of important arguments and positions that emerged later in the history of philosophy. All of the great thinkers of the Western tradition read Augustine, and they found valuable things in his work—whether they ultimately agreed with him or not.

2
Theodicy

The word "theodicy" is a combination of the two Greek words *"theos"* and *"dike,"* which mean "god" and "justice," respectively. A theodicy is an attempt to justify God's tolerance of evil.

Most people consider the existence of evil to be an obvious fact about the world. Evil includes two basic categories. First, there are evil actions, such as insulting a friend or torturing a child. Second, there are natural evils, such as earthquakes and viruses. We call both categories "evil" because, in both, innocent people are hurt, or, more generally, beautiful things are destroyed.

Augustine's search for a theodicy was motivated by personal experience. Not only did he live during a very tumultuous period in history, he also suffered a great deal in his own life. He wanted to believe in God, but he felt that he could only believe if he understood why God tolerated so much evil. In exploring the nature of God's justice, Augustine developed solutions to the problem of evil that would dominate Western thought ever after.

2.1 The Problem of Evil

The problem of evil arises for anyone who believes in an omnipotent, omniscient, and omnibenevolent deity. How is the existence of such a being consistent with the existence of evil? The problem is stated more formally in the following argument:

1. Evil exists.
2. If God does not know about evil, then He is not omniscient.
3. If God does know about evil but cannot prevent it, then he is not omnipotent.

4. If God does know about evil and can prevent it but does not do so, then he is not omnibenevolent.

The conclusion is that the existence of evil proves that there cannot be an omniscient, omnipotent, and omnibenevolent deity.

Many philosophers throughout history have turned to atheism precisely because they think the problem of evil presents an irrefutable argument. Of course, the problem of evil arises only in a monotheistic religion that invests all of the various powers and perfections in a single being. For pantheists or pagans, the problem need not arise. When considered in connection with Christianity, however, the argument can be very convincing.

The first premise seems self-evident (although we will see Augustine attempt to deny it). The second and third premises seem to be true by definition. The two most common responses, therefore, focus on the fourth premise.

One common response to the fourth premise is the freedom response. It holds that evil is the price of human freedom. In his benevolence, God wanted to create a world without evil. In his wisdom, however, he knew that human beings could not be happy unless they were free to live their own lives. Like a good parent, God allows us to live our own lives, and in so doing, he opens the door to both kinds of evil. Evil *actions* are directly caused by human choices. *Natural* evils are indirectly caused by human choices. After all, there is nothing evil about an earthquake or a virus unless a human being stumbles into it. God would not allow us to stumble into evil if we chose to listen to him. On this view, God is not responsible for evil because all evil is the direct or indirect consequence of human choice.

The other common response to the fourth premise is the agnostic response. It holds that God's wisdom so transcends our understanding that what appears to us as evil is not really evil after all. Inspiration for this view comes from the Old Testament Book of *Job*. In this book, God tests his faithful servant Job by inflicting plague after plague upon him. Job prays and listens to God, but God continues to test him. Finally, Job asks God to justify his actions. In response, God thunders, "Where were you when I made the world?" —in effect reminding Job that it is not for the finite mind of humans to know the infinite mind of God. On this view, a true theodicy is impossible because, although God is just, his justice is incomprehensible to us.

Augustine was perhaps the first philosopher in Western history to systematize these two responses. Early in his career he develops the first response, but by the end of his life, he resorts to the second.

2.2 Libertarianism and Determinism

The freedom response states that God made human beings free, and constructed the world in such a way that when they do other than what they should do, they suffer evil. The main task Augustine faces, therefore, is to prove that freedom is a real feature of human existence and that it consists in our ability to do other than we ought.

This is a more difficult task than one might expect. Philosophers have been debating the nature and existence of human freedom for a very long time. Two dominant positions have emerged.

Metaphysical libertarianism is the view Augustine needs. It holds that human beings have the power to act freely. A free action is an action that is not determined by antecedent conditions outside of the agent's will. Imagine that a doctor's patient, sitting calmly on the examining table, suddenly kicks her leg. This act would be free, according to the libertarian, only if the patient was able both to kick and not to kick before she did it. If antecedent conditions made it impossible for her to refrain from kicking (the doctor tapped her knee with a rubber hammer, say), then the act was not free. Libertarians are generally happy to admit that not all human action is free, but they maintain that some human action is free. In fact, they insist that we are not justified in judging humans to be responsible for an action unless it is free.

Determinism is the opposing view. It holds that no human action is free. Rather, everything that happens in the universe is caused by antecedent conditions, and could not have been otherwise. Any number of things might cause our patient to kick her leg. It might be a reflex, it might be anger, it might be a desire to get someone's attention, etc. Whether it is a belief, an emotion, or a physical force, some factor or combination of factors caused that action. This is to say that, given the presence of those factors, the patient was not able not to kick her leg. She may *feel* that she was able not to, but this is only because she was not aware of all the factors causing her to do what she did.

Libertarianism is the common sense view that most people come to believe on the basis of personal experience. We feel that we are sometimes free, so why suppose we are not?

There are many reasons to doubt the experience of freedom. Anyone who wants to develop a comprehensive picture of the universe will soon run into difficulties making sense of the ability to do otherwise.

Consider the matter from Aristotle's point of view. He was a pagan who conceived of God as the Unmoved Mover, a concept preserved in the Christian tradition. Aristotle's cosmology implies that God is the only thing in the universe that that moves without being moved by something else. Every human action, even a decision, is a kind of motion. Therefore, even a decision is moved by something else. This chain of movers is an unbroken chain of causes. To insist upon human freedom would be to envision breaks in the causal chain: miniature unmoved movers creating individual histories. This leaves us without a single explanation for the history of the universe as a whole. Many systematic thinkers prefer to assume that determinism is true.

It is sometimes argued that contemporary human sciences, particularly biology and psychology, presuppose determinism, or at the very least, that these sciences are more at home in the determinist camp. The task of these sciences is in part to explain human behavior in terms of antecedent physical and social conditions, and their success is quite remarkable. We can now chemically control and alter many of the choices people make. Since the feeling of freedom still accompanies these "choices," this might be taken as evidence that the feeling of freedom is an illusion.

In the dialogues *Phaedrus* and *Timaeus*, Plato provides some precedent for resisting this deterministic view. He conceived of God as the Demiurge who created the universe by bringing order to a pre-existing chaos. He also thought human beings are like God in so far as they bring order to their own souls. He describes the human soul through an analogy. Imagine a chariot driven by a charioteer and drawn by two steeds, one light, and one dark. The light horse represents the honorable part of the soul, the dark horse represents the naughty part of the soul, and the charioteer represents the part of the soul that controls these conflicting impulses. The charioteer directs the horses without himself being directed by anything else. This would seem to be a promising model for libertarianism. Plato never succeeded, however, in translating the analogy into a workable theory.

The problem is that libertarianism implies that human beings have a Godlike power. Augustine needs a strong metaphysical hypothesis to support this theory.

2.3 The Invention of the Will?

It is commonly asserted that Augustine was the first philosopher to introduce a full-blown concept of will. The will is the facet of the mind that makes human beings free.

Libertarians often describe the will as a power by which we exempt ourselves from the laws of nature. Gravity pulls rocks down; sunlight and nitrogen lift trees up; instinct causes squirrels to bury nuts— none of these things can do other than they do. Libertarians admit that human beings are subject to certain natural impulses as well, such as the need to eat, sleep, and copulate. A human being, however, by sheer force of will, can resist such impulses. In addition to defying nature, we have the power to go beyond nature by inventing a goal for ourselves or consciously breaking a tie between competing goals. This is what libertarians mean when they assert that human beings have free will.

The Latin word for will is "*voluntas*." Although this word was in currency long before Augustine, no one had ever put it to work in metaphysics quite the way he did.

Augustine's first clue to the existence of the will came from personal experience. In *Confessions*, he writes:

...I now was as much aware that I had a will as that I had a life. And when I willed to do or not do anything, I was quite certain that it was myself and no other who willed, and I came to see that the cause of my sin lay there. But what I did unwillingly, it seemed to me that I rather suffered than did, and I judged it to be not my fault but my punishment.... [D 109-10]

Augustine is correct that we do at least seem to have direct evidence of the existence of free will through introspection. On the other hand, it is open to the determinist to respond that there is a big difference between *knowing* something exists and *believing* something exists. So far, Augustine has done nothing to disprove the determinist's claim that freedom is an illusion.

In an early work called *On Free Choice of the Will*, however, Augustine offers an argument. It begins with the question, how do good human beings turn bad? An extended discussion leads Augustine to the answer that only free will can account for this phenomenon. He writes,

The conclusions that we have reached thus far indicate that a mind that is in control, one that possesses virtue, cannot be made a slave to inordinate desire by anything equal or superior to it, because such a thing would be just, or by anything inferior to it, because such a thing would be too weak. Just one possibility remains: only its own will and free choice can make the mind a companion of cupidity. [H 17]

The logic of this argument, which we will call "the virtuous mind argument," is not hard to follow. We should examine it in detail.

First, Augustine considers the possibilities. If something causes a virtuous mind to lose its virtue, that thing is either inside the mind or outside the mind. If it is outside the mind, then it is either superior to it, equal to it, or inferior to it.

Second, Augustine asserts that anything superior or equal to a virtuous mind could not cause it to lose its virtue. Here he is assuming that the only thing that could be superior or equal to a virtuous mind would be another virtuous mind, and that a virtuous mind would have to be just. He further assumes that a just mind, being just, could not cause another mind to lose its virtue.

Third, Augustine claims that anything inferior to a virtuous mind could not cause it to lose its virtue. Here he assumes that anything that is inferior would also be weaker. This implies that it could not cause the virtuous mind to lose its virtue because it would have to be at least as strong as that mind to do so.

These three premises taken together establish that nothing outside a virtuous mind can cause it to lose its virtue. Therefore, something inside the virtuous mind must cause this—namely, the will. As Augustine famously asks, "what is so much in the power of the will as the will itself?" [H 19]

This conclusion is libertarian because when Augustine says that it is the will that can "make the mind a companion to cupidity," he means that the will is the sole cause of sin, i.e., that the will causes sin without itself being caused by anything else. He writes,

> But perhaps you are going to ask what is the source of this movement by which the will turns away from the unchangeable good toward a changeable good. . . . If I told you that I don't know, you might be disappointed; but that would be the truth. For one cannot know that which is nothing. [H 69]

Nothing causes the will. The will is an uncaused cause, an unmoved mover. Augustine is not embarrassed to admit this because he sees himself as putting end to a vicious infinite regress. He writes,

> The will is the cause of sin, but you are asking about the cause of the will itself. Suppose that I could find this cause. Wouldn't we then have to look for the cause of this cause? What limit will there be on this search? Where will our questions and discussions end? [H 104]

Through the virtuous mind argument, Augustine has already shown why the end of the line of questioning has to lie within the individual mind. He sees no point in positing some further cause within the individual mind to explain what causes the will to move because then he would simply need to posit yet another cause within the mind to explain what causes the first cause to move, and so on ad infinitum.

14

The most puzzling thing about the virtuous mind argument is Augustine's use of the measurements "superior," "equal," and "inferior." He proceeds as though these measurements are as objective and observable as "taller," "same height," and "shorter." But it is not clear that they are. Height refers to a scale that can be measured in inches or centimeters. On what scale are "superior," "equal," and "inferior" measured? Is there any such scale?

Neoplatonists believed that there is. In order to understand fully what Augustine was trying to accomplish in the virtuous mind argument we need to examine the neoplatonic belief in a scale of measurement called the great chain of being.

2.4 The Great Chain of Being

The great chain of being is a scale of measurement for existence itself.

Most people today think of existence as an all-or-nothing affair: either you exist or you do not. For example, the Earth, Cher, and this book all exist, whereas unicorns and the Starship Enterprise do not. Existence is either "off" or "on," just like the light in a room with a standard light switch.

Neoplatonists, in contrast, would compare existence to the light in a room with a dimmer switch. There are degrees of existence, and each thing in the universe can be measured according to how much existence it has. Things with more existence are superior on the great chain of being, things with less are inferior on that scale. If talking in terms of degrees of existence or reality sounds odd, one might also capture the idea of the great chain of being by talking about degrees of perfection, complexity, or even degrees of potency.

The origin of this idea can be found in Plato. According to Plato's cosmology, the matter out of which things are made has always existed. The Demiurge created the world as we know it by giving form to the matter. The Demiurge did not, however, fashion each thing individually. Rather, he had a stock of basic forms to use—rather like cookie cutters on cookie dough. This explains why the things in this world come in kinds. For example, although there is a multitude of human beings, each one slightly different, they are all recognizable as members of humankind. According to Plato, they are the same kind because they were made from the same basic form. Likewise for all the other kinds of things found in this world.

Although this makes for a nice creation myth, philosophers pressed Plato for details. Did he really mean to say that there is a form for each and every kind of thing? What about hair, mud, and fingernails? Does the Demiurge have a cookie cutter for each of those?

In response to criticism along these lines, Plato developed the thesis that there is actually only one basic form, namely, the form of the good. All of the kinds of things we see in the world are made from aspects of the form of the good. Human beings have a large portion of the form of the good in them. Hair and fingernails have less, since they are only proper parts of human beings. Mud hardly has any of the form of the good in it at all, since mud is not all that different from the primordial matter out of which things are made.

Neoplatonists took Plato's idea to imply that each thing in the world has a degree of existence that exactly matches its degree of goodness. Considered as a lump of primordial matter, something either exists or does not exist, but considered as a kind of thing in this world, it exists in degrees. Kinds that have more of the form of the good in them exist to a greater degree than kinds that have less.

Augustine not only accepts this neoplatonic picture, but also uses it to motivate a basic causal principle. This principle appears often in Augustine's thinking. It also plays a prominent role in the works of other philosophers, most notably, René Descartes (1596-1650). We will call it the neoplatonic causal principle.

Neoplatonic Causal Principle: In order for one thing, x, to have causal power over another thing, y, x must exist to an equal or greater degree than y.

The more existence a thing has the more causal power it has.

This background affords us an analysis of Augustine's virtuous mind argument. A virtuous mind has a lot of the form of the good in it, and hence exists to a fairly high degree. Something that has less of the form of the good in it (i.e., something that is inferior) exists to a lesser degree, and hence has no causal power over that mind. Something that does have causal power over the virtuous mind, in contrast, exists to an equal or greater degree, but in that case, it has more of the form of the good in it as well (i.e., it is superior). Something with more form of the good than a virtuous mind cannot be so unjust as to cause a virtuous mind to lose its virtue. Augustine concludes that the only thing that can cause a virtuous mind to lose its virtue is its own free choice.

2.5 Divine Culpability

It is a matter of dispute whether or not the virtuous mind argument successfully establishes that human beings have the freedom to choose between good and evil. Supposing, however, that it does, would this mean that Augustine has vindicated the freedom response to the problem of evil?

The most pressing objection asserts that the freedom response does not absolve God of responsibility for the evil in the world because causality is transitive. Augustine insists that it is human beings that cause evil. Nevertheless, he also admits that God caused human beings. And God knew full well ahead of time that human beings were going to cause evil. By transitivity, God is the ultimate cause of evil. Why, therefore, is he not culpable?

An analogy helps to illustrate the point. Suppose Dr. Frankenstein builds a device that he knows will kill. Should we blame the device for the inevitable deaths, or should we blame Dr. Frankenstein? It seems clear that we should blame Dr. Frankenstein: it is morally irrelevant that he did not do the deeds directly.

This objection gains further momentum from the fact that God is standing by as the evil consequences of our choices play themselves out. Suppose you are watching as an innocent bystander is harmed. Most people believe that, if you are able, you should try to prevent this. Yet God does not prevent the evils that result from our choices.

In the end, the divine culpability objection asks, why did God fail to build human beings with enough intelligence and compassion so that, although they were free to choose evil, they never would?

To his credit, Augustine saw this objection more clearly than many later philosophers, and went some distance toward answering it. His strategy will be to use the famous neoplatonic thesis of the non-existence of evil to deny that the case of Dr. Frankenstein is analogous to the case of God. On this view, evil is not a positive entity like Dr. Frankenstein's killing device. Rather, evil is a nothingness, and nothingness is a necessary condition for the existence of any positive entities at all. Augustine writes,

> Now what is the so-called evil but a privation of the good? In the bodies of animals affliction with diseases and wounds is nothing other than the privation of health. For, when a cure is worked, it does not mean that those evils which were present, that is, the diseases and the wounds, recede thence and are elsewhere; they simply are not. For a wound or a disease is not a substance, but a vice of the fleshly substance; the substance, surely something good, is flesh itself, its accidents being the aforementioned evils, that is, privations of that good which is called health. In like manner evils in the soul are privations of natural good. When they are cured,

17

they are not transferred to another place; since they can have no place in the healthy soul, they can be nowhere. [L, IV, 376-7] Although Augustine does not deny that evil happens, he does deny that these happenings are things. He therefore can be seen as challenging premise one of the original argument for the problem of evil. According to Neoplatonism, the loss of virtue is a loss of some of the form of the good, and hence a loss of existence itself. No wonder, then, that the misuse of freedom makes human beings miserable. It makes us inferior and hence weaker in every way. To suffer evil, in the neoplatonic system is to suffer non-being. God cannot be held responsible for causing evil to exist because evil is not an existing reality. Rather, it is like the hole in a donut: an emptiness implied by the structure of the thing.

In light of the fact that we are so full of holes, it may seem better that human beings were never created. Augustine insists, however, that this would be too hasty a conclusion. After all, only God can be absolutely perfect, and he cannot create himself. Therefore, when he creates, he necessarily creates something less than absolutely perfect. This does not mean it is not good. Augustine writes,

> All natural beings are good, since the Creator of every one of them is supremely good . . . So long as a being is in process of corruption, there is present in it a good of which it is being deprived . . . Every being, therefore, is good—a great good if it cannot be corrupted; a small one if it can: but only the foolish and ignorant would deny that it is good. And if a being is consumed by corruption, then neither will the corruption remain, no being subsisting there where it can find a place. [L, IV, 377]

God could have created beings that are free and yet never choose evil. In fact, he did—they are called angels, and they are one rung above us on the great chain of being. The excellence of the angels can only be realized, however, as part of a bigger picture, a picture that includes the whole range of existences. These existences are ordered on the great chain of being as follows:

God: eternal, sinless, rational, living, beautiful
Angels: sinless, rational, living, beautiful
Humans: rational, living, beautiful
Animals: living, beautiful
Light: beautiful

Everything in the universe falls somewhere on this scale, each element being necessary to complete the grand scheme of things.

Augustine considers the varying degrees of existence among things to be like degrees of brightness in the starry sky. He writes,

> When you observe the differences among [them] and see that some are brighter than others, it would be wrong to want to get rid of the darker ones, or to make them just like the brighter ones. Instead, if you refer all of them to the perfection of the whole, you will see that these differences in brightness contribute to the more perfect being of the universe. The universe would not be perfect unless the greater things were present in such a way that the lesser things are not excluded. [H 88]

The universe as a whole is as perfect as it could be, even though individual members of the universe are not as perfect as they could be. In saying this, Augustine lays the groundwork for the claim, made famous by Gottfried Leibniz (1646-1716), that this world is the "Best of all Possible Worlds."

Are these moves sufficient to meet the divine culpability objection? Some philosophers continue to work on refinements to the freedom response and are committed to one or another version of it. Others remain unconvinced, perhaps because the conception of evil as a negation or privation just seems like a counterintuitive result resting on sophistical semantics. What is important for our purposes is that Augustine himself became deeply dissatisfied with it over time. As he experienced more of life, and as he discovered more about the religious tradition he was inheriting, he slowly realized that he would have to move away from libertarianism and the freedom response, and toward determinism and the agnostic response instead.

2.6 Grace

Writing his *Retractations* at the end of his life, Augustine looks back on his early treatment of the problem of evil with some regret. He writes, "In the solution of this question, I, indeed, labored in defense of the free choice of the human will; but the grace of God conquered . . . " [L, LX, 120]

Grace is unconstrained and undeserved divine favor. Christians often use this concept to explain miraculous transformations in their lives: conversion, healing, sudden insight, etc. Grace is deeply entrenched in the Judeo-Christian tradition, and Augustine himself felt that he had experienced it. There is a tension between grace and free will because grace provides an alternative explanation of how human beings are able to defy and transcend nature.

Which was it that caused Augustine to retract his libertarianism: his experience of grace or his concern to vindicate the Judeo-Christian tradition? We may never know.

What we do know is that, after Augustine published *On Free Choice of the Will*, a splinter group began forming within the Catholic Church. They were known as Pelagians, named after Pelagius (c. 360-c. 462), an English monk who settled in Rome. Pelagians claimed to be able to attain moral perfection in this life through sheer force of will. Relying on ambiguous Biblical texts for support, they asserted that human beings could earn their way into heaven, thereby constraining God to reward them. The Catholic Church soon officially condemned their view as heresy.

Much to Augustine's dismay, Pelagians cited certain passages of *On Free Choice of the Will* in their defense. For example, Augustine states that, "it is by the will that we lead and deserve a praiseworthy and happy life, or a contemptible and unhappy one." [H 22] Clearly, Pelagians were somewhat justified in considering Augustine one of their own.

Pelagius made a strategic mistake, however, when he publicly compared Augustine's African accent and manners to those of a braying donkey. In so doing, he acquired an avid enemy for himself and for the freedom of the will. Augustine decided that he had plenty of reasons for championing grace instead.

First, he had his own personal experience. There is a salient fact about life that Augustine came to feel libertarianism could not explain. Human beings are subject to bad habits and urges that lead us to act contrary to our intentions.

Consider, for example, the kleptomaniac, the alcoholic, the lecher, the smoker, the procrastinator, the spendthrift, the nail-biter, the over-eater, the potty-mouth, the space-cadet, the kill-joy, and any number of other personalities with which most of us are intimately familiar. Sometimes people with these personalities do not even realize what they are doing. Worse yet, sometimes they know perfectly well what they are doing but still cannot stop. Augustine repeatedly cites himself as an example. Addressing himself in *Soliloquies*, he writes,

> How vile, how detestable, how shameful, how dreadful did we
> consider the embrace of a woman, when we were making an in-
> quiry between ourselves concerning the desire for a wife! Yet that
> same night while we were lying awake and going over these things
> once more in our minds, you realized how differently from your

claims those imagined caresses and their bitter sweetness excited you. [L, I, 376]

Augustine admits that he has been enslaved to sexual desire all his life, even after his conversion and ordination.

Augustine called this sort of problem "ignorance and difficulty." He became convinced that ignorance and difficulty is not just an occasional problem in humans, but rather, their defining characteristic. We enslave ourselves to debilitating patterns. When and if we finally break out of such patterns, it seems like a miracle that comes from the outside. This led Augustine to doubt the reality of human freedom.

Second, he had the Bible. When Augustine began studying Scripture for his sermons, he found texts suggesting that every positive power human beings have is nothing but God working through us. He also found texts suggesting that God purposefully inflicts us with ignorance and difficulty in order to provide an opportunity for the gift of divine grace.

The turning point in Augustine's thinking on this issue can be traced to his famous exegesis of the New Testament text of Romans 9. [See Augustine's letter to Simplician in F] In Romans 9, the apostle Paul is discussing the Old Testament incident in which Rebecca bears twin sons, Jacob and Esau. Jacob grows up to become a great leader of the Israelites and Esau grows up to be a disgrace. Paul indicates that the point of this story is to show that God does not save human beings as a reward for good works. This is evident from the fact that God loved Jacob and hated Esau while they were still an undifferentiated lump of matter in the womb. Nor did God choose Jacob over Esau because he foresaw that the former would be good and the later would be wicked. Rather, Jacob's good fortune was the result of unconstrained and undeserved divine favor. Biblical passages like this one convinced Augustine that grace functions, not just as an occasional lift, but as the ultimate determinant of our lives.

Until his dying day, Augustine denied that he ever was a Pelagian. Concerning the suspicious passages of *On Free Choice of the Will*, he writes,

> In these and similar treatments of mine, because there was no mention of the grace of God, which was not the subject under discussion at the time, the Pelagians think or may think that we held their opinion. But they are mistaken in thinking this. For it is precisely the will by which one sins and lives rightly, a subject we discussed here. Unless this will, then, is freed by the grace of God from the servitude by which it has been made a "servant of sin,"

and unless it is aided to overcome its vices, mortal men cannot live rightly and devoutly. [L, LX, 35]

Augustine comes to see the human mind less in terms of freedom and more in terms of bondage as he grows older. In so doing, he develops the doctrine of original sin.

2.7 Original Sin

Original sin is the sin that all human beings have inherited from their original parents, Adam and Eve. It complements the concept of grace by explaining why it is that we are unable to escape ignorance and difficulty by ourselves.

According to Augustine, evil consists in suffering, and suffering consists in ignorance and difficulty. Whether you are dealing with your own urges, someone else's urges, or the ebb and flow of nature itself, the problem is that you do not understand the phenomenon well enough, and even if you did, you would not be able to do anything about it. So far, Augustine has offered a fairly perceptive, and perhaps even accurate, description of the misery involved in human existence.

But why is human existence this way? This is the question Augustine was determined from the very beginning to answer. The freedom response holds that human beings bring this suffering upon ourselves by choosing not to do what we should. On this view, ignorance and difficulty is an individual punishment for individual wrongs.

There is a clear challenge to this claim, however, in the case of infants. It seems that infants suffer ignorance and difficulty before they can possibly have the opportunity to abuse their freedom.

Augustine vaguely recognizes this problem in *On Free Choice of the Will*. There he attempts to explain infant suffering in virtue of its role in punishing others. He writes,

> Since God achieves some good by correcting adults through the
> suffering and death of children who are dear to them, why
> shouldn't such things take place? Once the suffering is past it will
> be for the children as if they had never suffered. . . . Who knows
> what a reward God has prepared for them in the hidden depths of
> his judgment? [H 117]

Augustine was never quite convinced by this explanation, however. Obviously, the question is why the *innocent* have to suffer in order to punish the guilty. Causing the suffering of other guilty ones who are dear to the sinner could accomplish the same goal. This problem continued to worry Augustine, and he soon realized that, if his theodicy was to survive, it would have to solve the problem of infant suffering.

The whole problem is that it seems as though infants are innocent. If they are innocent, then they should not suffer. But what if they are not innocent after all? In *Confessions*, Augustine presents a new picture of childhood. He writes,

> I have myself seen a small baby jealous; it was too young to speak, but it was livid with anger as it watched another infant at the breast. There is nothing unusual in this. Mothers and nurses will tell you that they have their own way of curing these fits of jealousy. But at any rate it is an odd kind of innocence when a baby cannot bear that another—in great need, since upon that one food his very life depends—should share the milk that flows in such abundance. [D 8]

Such examples demonstrate to Augustine that babies are not innocent.

It is still undeniable, however, that babies often suffer, and suffer deeply, before they are able to make any choices. This is the greatest challenge of all to the freedom response to the problem of evil. The freedom response presupposes that bad choices are punished individually. Augustine realized that the only way to account for infant suffering is to suppose instead that bad choices are punished communally.

This is precisely the motive behind the doctrine of original sin. Original sin posits communal guilt. Because the human race has sinned, the human race is guilty—individual identities are irrelevant. Augustine claims to have found this doctrine in the Bible, though he was accused, during his own lifetime, of inventing it. Nor does he claim to understand it very clearly. How is the guilt transmitted? Augustine admits that he does not know. All he knows is that God must allow human beings to experience ignorance and difficulty from conception because we are all somehow guilty from conception. And the corollary of this doctrine is infant damnation: anyone who is not baptized and absolved of sin before dying goes straight to hell.

This may seem an extreme response to the problem of infant suffering. It has been widely criticized for attributing to God a method of punishment more appropriate to the most egregious dictator, and one that not even the strictest of parents would consider adopting. Augustine, however, is not concerned. He writes,

> Indeed all sinful souls have been afflicted with these two punishments: ignorance and difficulty. Because of ignorance, error warps our actions; because of difficulty, our lives are a torment and an affliction . . .But here we come across the slanderous question that is

so often asked by those who are ready to blame their sins on anything but themselves: "If it was Adam and Eve who sinned, what did we poor wretches do? How do we deserve to be born in the blindness of ignorance and the torture of difficulty?" . . . My response is brief: let them be silent and stop murmuring against God. [H 107]

In the end, the problem of infant suffering is the decisive factor that pushed Augustine away from the freedom response and toward the agnostic response. God's justice is simply beyond human understanding.

2.8 Divine Morality

It is important to realize the significance of this move. In resorting to the agnostic response, Augustine surrenders his search for a theodicy. He set out to "justify the ways of God to man," and has come to the conclusion that it cannot be done. Omnibenevolence is inscrutable. On the one hand, this enables Augustine to solve the problem of evil once and for all. No matter how bad life becomes, it will not prove that God does not exist. On the other hand, the question arises why anyone should believe in such a God. Once justification is lost, one might as well suppose that human suffering is a result of random chance.

What exactly does it mean, though, to say that justification is lost? A distinction needs to be made between strong agnosticism and weak agnosticism. The weak agnostic maintains that there definitely is a justification for human suffering, but we just cannot know what it is. The strong agnostic maintains not only that we cannot know the justification but that there is none, because God is above and beyond justification. It is not always clear which version of the agnostic response Augustine is committed to.

There is an objection, however, that covers both versions. It holds that both weak and strong agnosticism portray God as acting in a way that most people find immoral.

We can see this through an analogy. Suppose you are born with a heritable disease. In the current state of technology, it would be absurd for you to blame your parents. While it is true that they caused you to have that trait, there was nothing they could do about it. The revolution in genetics that is now unfolding, however, may change things. Suppose your parents easily could have prevented you from inheriting the disease but did not. You ask them why, only to find that they have no justification whatsoever. This seems outrageously immoral. Alternately, suppose they claim that there is a justification but that you could never understand it. Once again, this seems morally unacceptable. And yet this seems exactly analogous to the case of God. Why should moral judgements that apply to human beings not apply to God?

Most philosophers today believe that moral judgements do apply to God, and that part of what makes God omnibenevolent is that he does the most moral thing possible on every occasion. They will have to work harder to find a satisfactory solution to the problem of evil. (For a survey of recent discussions of the problem of evil, see Marilyn McCord Adams and Robert Merrihew Adams, *The Problem of Evil*, Oxford, 1990.)

There is another way of looking at the matter, however. If you suppose that moral judgements apply to God, then you are presupposing that there is a moral standard that exists independently of God. But what is that standard? And by what further standard should that standard be identified and judged? This line of reasoning quickly leads to an infinite regress. Divine command theorists avoid this problem. They hold that God is the end to the regress. There is no moral standard independently of him. Since what he does defines what is moral, what he does cannot coherently be judged as immoral.

Augustine is committed to divine command theory for other reasons anyway. Hence, he may have a response to the divine morality objection. Nevertheless, he was never able to resuscitate a plausible account of human freedom.

2.9 Compatibilism

Augustine's later reliance on the concepts of grace and original sin turn him into a determinist of the theological variety. Theological determinists hold that everything we do is caused by antecedent conditions, ultimately traceable to God. Although the later Augustine is clearly a theological determinist, it is more accurate to attribute to him the "soft" version of determinism known as compatibilism. Compatibilism is the view that, although all human actions are caused by antecedent conditions, it is still appropriate to call some of them "free."

Compatibilists want to distinguish actions that are internally caused from actions that are externally caused. Consider, once again, the case of our patient suddenly kicking her leg. Suppose that what caused her to do this was that her physician tapped her reflex. This would mean that the action was externally caused, and hence should not be considered free. Suppose, on the other hand, that what caused her to kick her leg was a desire for attention. According to the compatibilist, this would still be an antecedent condition that made it impossible for her to refrain from kicking her leg. So, she was not free in the libertarian sense. Nevertheless, the compatibilist would call the action "free" in so far as it was internally caused. *Someone else* did not cause the patient to kick her leg; she did it of her own accord.

Compatibilists make this distinction because they want to hold human beings morally responsible only for their "free" (i.e. internally caused) actions. If something outside the patient caused her to kick her leg, then she cannot take the blame for it; if something inside her caused this, then she must take responsibility for it, even though she could not do otherwise.

Augustine is most charitably interpreted as a compatibilist. He, like most compatibilists, retains the language of free will because he knows that it is impossible to explain the human condition without it. Nevertheless, he commandeers this language to his own deterministic purposes. He wants to maintain that human beings cannot take credit for being good. The reason is that all good actions are caused by God's grace, an external cause. At the same time, he wants to maintain that human beings must take credit for being bad. The reason is that all bad actions are caused by our own wills. Since the will is an internal cause, we are responsible, even though we cannot do otherwise.

In his latest works, Augustine devotes himself to disparaging the alleged human dignity of free will and criticizing anyone who takes pride in it. He writes that human beings are "enslaved to sin," and that the best thing that can happen to us is to receive grace and thereby become "enslaved to God" instead.

Augustine's theodicy therefore makes a dubious contribution to the history of philosophy. On the one hand, it provides us with a personal yet intellectual confrontation with the problem of evil. On the other hand, it introduces the concept of free will, only to generate another set of concepts, grace and original sin, which cancel out any meaningful application of the concept of free will. In this way, Augustine reflects and reinforces the profound ambivalence toward human freedom that is endemic to Western thought.

3

Knowledge

Augustine found his salvation in religion. He was a classic "born again" Christian in many respects. It would be a mistake, however, to see him as an unthinking dogmatist. Augustine had always been an inquisitive person. He wanted to understand his life and the world around him. He came to Christianity because it had answers, answers that helped him make sense of things. We have already seen, for example, how it helped furnish a solution to the biggest problem on Augustine's mind: the problem of evil. This was not the only instance; over time, Augustine experienced that without God, all was darkness, and with God, everything became clear. He grew fond of the early (and, as it happens, inaccurate) translation of Isaiah 7:9: "Unless you believe, you will not understand." [See e.g., H 3, 32.] He interprets this passage to mean that philosophy builds a rational structure on the foundation of faith.

One of Augustine's first tasks as a philosopher was to justify his claim to have discovered some truths. There were plenty of philosophers then, as now, who denied that human beings can ever know anything for certain. Before he found religion, Augustine was inclined to agree. As a college student, he was much more impressed with the writings of Cicero, an Academic skeptic, than with scripture. [D 79] He even considered joining the Academic skeptics when he moved to Rome. But now he claimed to be a knower. What did he know? How did he know? Where did knowledge come from? Questions such as these provoked his interest in epistemology, the study of human knowledge. Augustine's epistemological theories inform many strands of Western thought.

3.1 Skepticism

The skepticism Augustine confronts has its roots in Plato's teacher, Socrates (470-399 B.C.). In Plato's *Apology*, Socrates claims that any wisdom he possesses consists in not thinking he knows what he does not know. Of course, this is not skepticism, but rather a prudent suspicion of intellectual pretensions, and Augustine would have had no quarrel with it. Plato's intellectual heirs, however, adapted the Socratic dictum, along with the Socratic method of questioning, to create two influential skeptical movements in the ancient world.

The milder, more palatable form of skepticism is Pyrrhonian skepticism, named after Pyrrho of Elis (c. 360 – c. 270 B.C.). The goal of the Pyrrhonian was to enjoy a state of *ataraxia*—happiness and contentment, which would arrive once one achieved *epoche*—suspension of belief or judgment. *Epoche* is produced by "tropes," a series of questions calculated to undermine one's beliefs.

Suppose you believe that the cover of the book in front of you is red. The Pyrrhonian skeptic might then ask you what color it would appear to a dog. You would reply that, since dogs are colorblind, the book would appear to them to be gray. Next, the skeptic would ask what color the book would appear to a Venusian equipped with infrared vision, or to Superman with x-ray eyes, or when viewed under ultra-violet light. In each case, you would give a different answer. The skeptic would then point out that there is no reason to think that you, one of countless different kinds of perceivers, have any kind of privileged access to the true color of the book. After all, you are a mere mortal, whose vision has never been perfect anyway.

In this way, the Pyrrhonian skeptic recommends being content with the way things seem, and not wasting time searching for truths behind the appearances. To some people in fourth-century North Africa, where there were so many competing theological and philosophical sects, all claiming to have discovered the ultimate nature of reality, this might have appeared to be a very attractive position. It is difficult to refute. Nevertheless, it did not tempt Augustine.

The other major strain of skepticism, the one that tempted Augustine, was known as Academic skepticism, named after Plato's Academy. Members of the Academy, most famously Carneades, first formulated this version of skepticism in the third century B.C. It was highly visible in Rome during Augustine's time, found in the writings of Cicero, Sextus Empiricus, and others. The Academic skeptics took Socrates' statement of intellectual humility and twisted it into the positive claim that we know that we know nothing at all.

The self-refuting nature of the statement "We know that we know nothing at all" is obvious. If we *really* know nothing then we cannot know that the statement is true.

Augustine belabors the point in his early work, *Against the Academicians.* He argues that Academic skeptics are ultimately trapped into asserting that the wise man does not know anything, "not even the very wisdom by reason of which he is called wise in the first place!" [A 68]

In effect, Augustine forces the Academic skeptics into a dilemma. Either they know that the wise man does not know anything or they do not know it. If they claim to know it, then they admit that they are wise, and hence do not know anything after all. If they claim not to know it, then they have no right to consider it true. Either way, they must abandon their position.

Carneades attempts to defend the Academic skeptics on the grounds that they do not consider the statements they believe in to be true, but rather, "truthlike." [A 49ff] Augustine replies that there are two ways of understanding this claim.

On the one hand, Carneades might mean "truth-like" in the literal sense. If so, then he must have some way of measuring how close to the truth the beliefs of the skeptics are. To be able to make such a measurement, however, one must have knowledge of the truth itself. In contemporary epistemology, this is known as the "problem of the criterion."

On the other hand, Carneades might be using the term "truth-like" as a placeholder for whatever the skeptics believe, regardless of how close to the truth these beliefs are. If so, then he is abusing language and does not deserve the courtesy of a reply. "Why then should we argue with someone who doesn't know how to express himself?" Augustine asks. [A 50]

Clearly, Academic skepticism is much easier to refute than is its Pyrrhonian cousin. Augustine wanted to maintain his neoplatonic conviction that it is possible to gain knowledge of ultimate reality. He realized that the only way to refute Pyrrhonean skepticism was to generate an account of the nature of knowledge.

3.2 Augustine's *Cogito*

In his *Meditations on First Philosophy*, published in 1641, the man known as the father of modern philosophy, René Descartes, famously proposes a method for conquering skepticism. His method is to try to convince himself that all of his beliefs are false. If he finds a belief of whose falsity he cannot be convinced, then he has found a belief that is certain, and immune to all doubt.

In order to aid his effort to convince himself that his beliefs are false, Descartes pretends that he has been deceived all his life by an evil genius. The evil genius has cleverly fooled him into believing that he has a body and that he lives in a material world, when in fact all of this is false. This thought experiment enables Descartes to go so far as to doubt, for a moment, his very own existence.

It is at this moment that a dramatic reversal takes place. Descartes realizes that the belief "I exist" is a belief that cannot be false. The very fact that the deceiver is deceiving him proves that he exists. Descartes writes,

> But there is some deceiver or other who is supremely powerful and supremely sly and who is always deliberately deceiving me. Then too there is no doubt that I exist, if he is deceiving me. And let him do his best at deception, he will never bring it about that I am nothing so long as I shall think that I am something. Thus, after everything has been most carefully weighed, it must finally be established that this pronouncement "I am, I exist" is necessarily true every time I utter it or conceive it in my mind. [N 18]

Descartes uses this famous argument, called "the *cogito*" from the Latin for "I think," to banish skepticism and lay a foundation of certainty for philosophy.

Now compare Augustine in *City of God*:

> In respect of those truths I have no fear of the arguments of the Academics. They say 'Suppose you are mistaken?' I reply, 'If I am mistaken, I exist.' A non-existent being cannot be mistaken; therefore I must exist, if I am mistaken. Then since my being mistaken proves that I exist, how can I be mistaken in thinking that I exist, seeing that my mistake establishes my existence? Since therefore I must exist in order to be mistaken, then even if I am mistaken, there can be no doubt that I am not mistaken in my knowledge that I exist. It follows that I am not mistaken in knowing that I exist. [C 460]

The resemblance is remarkable, and the same sort of formulation is found in *On Free Choice of the Will* [H 33]. Some translators even frame the argument in terms of deception.

Descartes was very secretive about his sources. When his friend and critic Antoine Arnauld (1612-94) remarked on how much Descartes' *cogito* resembled Augustine's, Descartes replied only that he was honored to have such a famous progenitor.

Augustine was like Descartes in using the *cogito* as a first positive step against the skeptics. When Pyrrhonian skeptics assert that the self is nothing more than an appearance, the *cogito* will soundly refute them. The *cogito* has an even broader significance for both Augustine and Descartes, however. It demonstrates that the source of true knowledge lies in thought. Those who are in doubt need only reflect upon their own doubt to find certainty again. The truth is innate within us.

3.3 Innatism and Empiricism

There have been two classic approaches to the problem of human knowledge throughout the history of philosophy, namely, empiricism, and innatism or rationalism.

Empiricism is the view that knowledge comes from the external world, as experienced through the five senses. According to empiricists, human beings are born with minds analogous to *tabula rasa*, blank slates. As babies, we are entirely ignorant. As we gain experience, we mechanically associate sense impressions with one another, and store the associated sense impressions as information in our minds.

Empiricism is a fairly common sense view. Serious problems arise, however, when you try to make sense of it philosophically.

One problem concerns self justification. The empiricist claims to know that all knowledge comes from experience. This raises the question: does the knowledge that all knowledge comes from experience *itself* come from experience? It seems highly unlikely. What would count as an experience of all knowledge coming from experience? It is difficult to see how knowledge of empiricism can itself be empirically justified. Some other justification of the empiricist stance will be required, and it is precisely this project that occupies a prominent contemporary empiricist, Bas C. van Fraassen (1941-).

Another problem is that strict empiricism leads to skepticism about the existence of the external world. George Berkeley (1685-1753) proves this as follows. Empiricists claim that all knowledge comes from sense impressions. They also claim that all sense impressions come from the external world. The question is this: how can they know the second claim to be true, given the first? In order to know that the external world causes sense impressions in them, they would need a sense impression of the external world causing sense impressions in them. But this is impossible. You would need to be outside of yourself in order to have sense impressions of yourself having sense impressions. Therefore, empiricists have no way of knowing whether their sense impressions come from an external world, or to what extent the veil of perception distorts reality.

Considering these and other difficulties with empiricism, it is not hard to see why Augustine pursued innatism instead. Innatism is the view that knowledge, at least important knowledge, comes from within. This might take the form, as with Immanuel Kant (1724-1804), of asserting that the mind imposes order and structure on the raw data of experience. Or it might take the form of positing innate ideas. Those who posit innate ideas deny the blank slate thesis. They claim that human beings are not born ignorant. Rather, we are born with truths implanted deep within our minds. Gaining knowledge does not require experience of the external world, but rather, reasoning about self-evident truths. This is the route Plato, Augustine, and later, Descartes will take.

One reason innatism is attractive is that it can escape what is known as the "paradox of learning." Plato first introduces the paradox of learning in his dialogue, *Meno*. It purports to show that learning would be impossible on the empiricist's "blank slate" model. If human beings were born ignorant, we would not be able to recognize the correct answers to our questions *as* the correct answers. Simply put, if you do not know what you are looking for, how will you know when you find it?

Augustine discusses the paradox in Book Ten of *Confessions*. He writes,

> The woman who had lost a groat sought it with a light. But she
> would not have found it if she had not remembered it. For when it
> was found, how should she have known whether it was what she
> sought, if she had not remembered it? ... We do not say that we
> have found what was lost unless we recognize it, nor can we rec-
> ognize it unless we remember. [D 186-7]

In this passage, Augustine shows how memory helps to address the paradox. If the thing you are looking for is something you have seen before, then you will have no trouble knowing it when you find it. But the question remains, how do human beings know it when they find a truth that they have never seen before?

Consider mathematical truths, for example. In *Meno*, Plato demonstrates that a boy who has no knowledge of geometry whatsoever can solve a complex geometrical problem. The boy discovers the theorem he needs through his own reasoning. How does he recognize it when he has never seen it before?

Plato's hypothesis is that what we call learning is really recollection of what we knew in a previous life. Plato conceives this previous life as a spiritual co-existence with the form of the good. The form of the good contains all truths. Our souls learned everything there is to know, therefore, before being born into a body. We need only remind ourselves.

Augustine declares himself agnostic on the previous life hypothesis. In his view, it is rash to speculate about when and how the soul and the body come together. In any case, the hypothesis of a previous life does not solve the problem. It only raises the question: how did we learn what we did in that previous life? Augustine develops a version of innatism designed to identify the ultimate source of learning.

3.4 Divine Illumination

Augustine's version of innatism is called divine illumination theory. It holds that God plants truths in our minds before birth and illuminates them when we ask questions and seek the truth.

Augustine makes his most sustained argument for this theory in a dialogue similar to *Meno* called *The Teacher*. The main goal of the work is to demonstrate that although teachers teach by using words, the words themselves cannot cause anyone to learn.

It may seem otherwise. Imagine a very common learning scenario. A teacher displays an array of novel items to a student, then names each item and explains what purpose it serves. The student has learned something, and it seems as though it was the teacher's words that taught her.

Augustine wants to deny this, however. The reason is that, according to Neoplatonism, it is impossible for words to have causal power over the mind. Recall from the last chapter that, as a corollary to his belief in the great chain of being, Augustine is committed to the following causal principle:

Neoplatonic Causal Principle: In order for one thing, x, to have causal power over another thing, y, x must exist to an equal or greater degree than y.

In order for words to have causal power over the mind they would have to exist to an equal or greater degree than the mind. Augustine claims in *The Teacher* that this is obviously false. Words, therefore, have no causal power over the mind.

Augustine does not only defend this view because his Neoplatonism entails it. He finds it to be evident from experience.

Consider again the case of the student. While listening to her teacher's explanations, she was all along consulting her own native intuitions: she imagined the new items in use; she asked herself, "Does what he is saying make sense?" Soon a voice in her mind answered "yes." Augustine calls this voice the Inner Teacher.

Augustine points out that without the Inner Teacher we would not know which words to accept and which to reject. He writes,

> For example, if I were to ask you about the very matter at issue, namely whether it's true that nothing can be taught by words, at first it would seem absurd to you, since you aren't able to examine it as a whole. It would therefore be necessary to ask you questions suited to your abilities to hear the Teacher within you. Thus I might say: "The things I'm saying that you admit to be truths, and that you're certain of, and that you affirm yourself to know— where did you learn them?" Maybe you would reply that I had taught them to you. Then I would rejoin: "What if I should say that I had seen a flying man? Do my words then make you as certain as if you were to hear that wise men are better than fools?" [A 141]

How do you know to accept the words, "Wise men are better than fools" and to reject the words, "A flying man exists"? Because the following truths are self-evident: something good is better than something bad, and that which is flightless cannot fly. The words serve only to remind you of these truths, not to cause them in you.

It might be objected that this analysis ignores the fact that words are symbols of thoughts. In the case of the student, it is not her teacher's words but his thoughts that seem to cause knowledge in her. The thesis that one person's thoughts can cause knowledge in another person would also be consistent with Neoplatonism. It is plausible to suppose that teacher's mind exists to an equal or greater degree than that of the student. It would therefore be possible for the teacher's mind to have causal power over the student.

Augustine refutes this objection by pointing out that adopting others' thoughts is not the same as gaining knowledge. He writes,

> Do teachers hold that it is their thoughts that are perceived and grasped rather than the very disciplines they take themselves to pass on by speaking? After all, who is so foolishly curious as to send his son to school to learn what the teacher thinks? When the teachers have explained by means of words all the disciplines they profess to teach, even the disciplines of virtue and of wisdom, then those who are called "students" consider within themselves whether truths have been stated. [A 145]

Students will not learn anything if they merely adopt their teachers' thoughts. They have to understand why their teachers' thoughts are true.

Although Augustine denies that learning consists in the teacher implanting thoughts in the student, this "implantation model" nevertheless provides him with an important clue.

The problem with the implantation model is that having a truth in one's mind does not make it knowledge. As every geometry teacher knows, it will not do any good simply to make the students memorize theorems. They have to use the theorems actively in order to understand them. If teachers could implant truths in the students' minds and then magically activate them, then they really could make students learn this way. Unfortunately, human beings do not have the power to activate truths in others' minds.

God, however, does. According to Augustine, he implants truths in the human mind and then illuminates them for us, so that we understand what they mean. The voice of the Inner Teacher is actually the voice of God. Augustine writes,

> For the Light is God Himself, whereas the soul is a creature; yet, since it is rational and intellectual it is made in His image. And when it tries to behold the Light, it trembles in its weakness and finds itself unable to do so. Yet from this source comes all the understanding it is able to attain. When, therefore, it is thus carried off and, after being withdrawn from the senses of the body, is made present to this vision in a more perfect manner (not by a spatial relation, but in a way proper to its being), it also sees above itself that Light in whose illumination it is enabled to see all the objects that it sees and understands in itself. [I, II, 222]

This is the doctrine of divine illumination.

Divine illumination accomplishes the same thing as Plato's theory of recollection, albeit in a different manner. Augustine indicates that divine illumination supplies the human mind with all of its ideas, whether these are reasoning patterns or conceptual categories. The ideas are copies of transcendent forms, and whereas Plato thought that these forms exist by themselves in the world of ideas, Augustine thought that they exist in the divine mind.

According to the view known as Mathematical Platonism, numbers and geometric shapes exist outside of the human mind. Augustine agrees. He writes that, although we rely on bodily senses to count things in the world, "the basic numbers *by* which we count are not the same as these, nor images of these; but really are." [D 182] Although

35

Augustine is a Platonist in that he thinks that numbers and the like exist outside of the human mind, he cannot quite assert that these realities are mind-independent because they exist in the divine mind.

3.5 Perception

One of the most pressing objections to Augustine's innatism concerns perception. It seems obvious that perception informs the mind about the world. This fact is not hard to understand on the empiricist view. Divine illumination theory, in contrast, seems incapable of explaining it. The same argument Augustine used to show that words have no causal power over the mind can be used to show that material objects have no causal power over the mind. After all, material objects fall lower on the great chain of being than minds do. Is perception, therefore, an illusion?

Augustine knew he would need a sophisticated argument in order to avoid this conclusion. He endeavors to develop an account of the human person that will enable him to explain perception.

Augustine's account of the human person is dualist. Dualism is the view that each human being is a composite of body and soul. Until very recently, dualism has been the dominant account of the human person in Western thought. One reason is that Christianity seems to require it: the soul of the human being is supposed to live on after the body dies. Many contemporary philosophers have turned to some version of materialism instead. Contrary to dualists, materialists claim that human beings are nothing but bodies. Hence, they are unable to accommodate the Christian belief in life-after-death. Wanting to resist this alternative, Christian philosophers have for a long time searched for an adequate account of the mind-body composite.

There is a famous problem involved in any such dualist account. The problem is encapsulated in the following question: how do the mind and the body interact?

Upon careful consideration, the problem becomes readily apparent. The body is a physical object. In order to move a physical object you must either push it or pull it. Therefore, in order to move the body, you must either push it or pull it. Yet, the only thing that can perform the task of pushing or pulling is another physical object. The soul is not a physical object. So how can it push or pull the body around?

It is easy to see how another physical object can interact with the body. If a car hits you and knocks you down, then we can identify, and even measure, the cause of the fall. But suppose instead that you throw yourself to the ground. How did your soul, without the physical properties required for pushing and pulling, cause your body to move in that way? Conversely, how can the physical cuts and gashes that you acquire in the fall cause the perception of pain in your soul? How does the body push or pull the soul into a state of pain? This problem, known in contemporary terms as the mind-body problem, makes dualism a difficult theory to defend.

Three main answers have been suggested throughout the history of philosophy. We sketch them briefly here in order to provide a background to Augustine's account.

One answer simply accepts the interaction as a primitive two-way causal relation. This view is called interactionism because it asserts that bodies and minds have a special power to interact, even though nothing much about this power is known or understood.

Another answer, parallelism, denies that body-soul interaction is possible. It asserts that bodies can only interact with bodies and souls can only interact with souls. It may look as though bodies interact with souls, as when you throw yourself to the ground. The parallelist maintains, however, that in such cases, the soul is acting in parallel to the body without any causal influence. This requires what is called a pre-established harmony between the actions of body and soul. A similar theory is occasionalism, developed by Nicolas Malebranche (1638-1715), which holds that physical interactions are occasions for God to effect changes in the soul.

Finally, there is epiphenomenalism. This view asserts one-way interaction: the body can have causal influence on the soul but not vice versa. On the one hand, epiphenomenalists agree with interactionists that the body causes the pain you feel in your soul when you acquire cuts and gashes. On the other hand, they agree with the parallelists that there is no need to suppose that your soul can throw your body to the ground. If your soul wants your body on the ground, this is just a parallel phenomenon.

Augustine's neoplatonic causal principle rules out each of these three traditional versions of dualism. It rules out two-way interactionism and epiphenomenalism because both of these theories maintain that physical objects have causal power over the soul. This cannot be according to the neoplatonist, since the soul is superior to physical objects on the great chain of being. The principle rules out parallelism because it maintains that that soul cannot have power over the body. This is false according to the neoplatonist, once again, because the soul is superior to physical objects on the great chain of being.

37

Augustine's Neoplatonism forces him to advance a fourth alternative. It is so rare in the history of philosophy that there is no name for it. We will call it "reverse-epiphenomenalism." Augustine asserts that the soul can have causal influence on the body, but not vice versa.

Augustine's commitment to reverse-epiphenomenalism clearly emerges when he is discussing perception. How is it that, when your eye is exposed to a certain object, your soul experiences the color red? Interactionists and epiphenomenalists would say that the red object causally affects the eyeball and then the eyeball causally affects the soul. This makes the soul passive during the process of perception.

Augustine, however, insists that the soul is always the active party. He agrees that the red object causally affects the eyeball. This is just a case of one body affecting another. What he denies is that the eyeball then affects the soul. Instead, he claims that the soul is all along activating the eyeball. Activating an eyeball that is seeing red is different from activating an eyeball that is seeing any other color. It is in virtue of this difference that the soul has a "perception" of red.

Augustine presents his reverse-epiphenomenalism in an early work called *On Music*. He writes,

> The body does not act on the soul, but the soul acts in relation to the body or in the body by the Divinely given mastery which it has over it. That may be more easy or less easy, according to the resistance offered by the bodily nature, which varies with the merit of each soul. External bodily events have effect on the body only, an effect which may either oppose or assist the work of the soul. When the soul has to strain against opposition, and finds difficulty in forcing its material to serve the causes of its own work, the very difficulty keys it up or makes it more intent, *fit attentior*, or alert, for action. So keyed up, it is aware of the difficulty, and this state of sensitivity is called perception. Perception itself is regarded as pain or effort. When the soul brings the body, which belongs to it into contact with an external body, which is in harmony with it, this action is perceived, because a new factor has been introduced, but the perception is pleasurable on account of the harmony. [J 91]

According to Augustine, a soul notices that it is perceiving one object rather than another because it is aware of itself: the activity of perceiving feels different in each case.

Augustine characterizes this difference in terms of ease and difficulty. An analogy with exercise helps clarify the point. Imagine that, right before your daily workout today, someone slips drug Z into your Gatorade. Drug Z has a strange power. It renders you completely unconscious for exactly one hour. When you become conscious again, you will be blind, deaf, and completely numb for exactly five minutes. The most amazing thing about drug Z is that it accomplishes all of this without interrupting its victim's day. After unknowingly ingesting drug Z, you proceed to your workout unconscious. You wake up an hour later doing the breaststroke in the pool. You are blind, deaf and completely numb. Yet, you can tell you are moving your body and you know you are swimming rather than walking. Why? Because swimming is more difficult than walking. Not only is swimming more difficult than walking, it is more difficult in a particular way. Perhaps swimming and running are equally difficult for you. Because they are difficult in different ways, however, you are aware of which you are doing. Suppose further that you sustained an injury while you were unconscious. You would know this as well before your senses revived because of the particular difficulty it would present to you.

It may seem odd to think that the soul gathers information from the world by feeling its own ease and difficulty. After all, it does not seem any more easy or difficult to see red rather than blue. Augustine might explain the peculiar difficulty of the five senses in terms of habit and expectation. For example, suppose that the ceiling in your room is white. Every morning when you wake up on your back you open your eyes to see white. Because you are expecting this, you no longer even notice the white. It is maximally easy. Likewise, when you travel to work, your eyes glance over many things you have seen many times before, but it is the new things that you notice. Why? Because they are comparatively difficult. Suppose you arrive at your office expecting to see your yellow door, but finds that the door has been painted blue instead. As Augustine put it, "the soul has to strain against opposition," and becomes more attentive to the activity on account of the difficulty. The same goes for hearing, smelling, tasting, and touching.

There may be some evidence for reverse-epiphenomenalism in everyday experience. Augustine was extremely interested in the fact that a person can read or listen to an entire page from a book without registering a word of it. The letters affected the eyes, the sounds affected the ears, but the soul was otherwise occupied. We might add to this another peculiar fact. The first time a tourist sees Mount Everest, the view is breathtaking. Nevertheless, the man who operates a motel in the nearby town hardly even sees the mountain any more. It is a common observation that any view "disappears" once you are used to it. Why is this? Perhaps because it ceases to exercise the soul.

39

The standard objection to views that portray the soul as the operator of the body, as does reverse-epiphenomenalism, is called the homunculus objection. The word "homunculus" means "little person" in Latin. Reverse-epiphenomenalism holds that you perceive that you are swimming because there is a little person inside you—the soul—who perceives its own difficulty. So the question arises: how does the soul perceive its own difficulty? It seems we need to posit another little person inside the soul, and then another little person inside that little person, and so on, to infinity.

Due to its lack of popularity throughout the history of philosophy, one suspects that there are more problems with reverse-epiphenomenalism than we are able to examine here. Nevertheless, it does provide Augustine with an answer to the charge that his epistemology leaves us without any explanation of perception.

3.6 Augustine's Ontological Proof

Another obvious objection to Augustine's epistemology is that it is completely dependent on the existence of God. In contemporary scientific theories of perception, or indeed in any scientific theory, using God is regarded as an *ad hoc* maneuver. It enables one to plug holes in theories that ought to be thrown out instead. In so far as epistemology is to regarded as scientific, then, it should not have to rely on the unproven hypothesis of the existence of God.

Augustine was sympathetic to this complaint. In his mature years, he admired "simple" Christians, like his mother, who devoted themselves to God without any proof. Like them, he had faith. At the same time, however, he felt that reason makes faith stronger. He wanted a strong foundation for his philosophy. He therefore deemed it important to try to prove that God exists.

Innatists and empiricists generally have very different approaches to proving the existence of God. While empiricists try to demonstrate that there is evidence of God in the external world, innatists argue that God's existence is self-evident. The innatist approach is called the "ontological" argument, after the Greek word for "being."

The ontological argument is perhaps the most notorious argument in the history of philosophy and theology. It is an argument that in one minute seems to be nothing but a trick of semantics and in the next minute seems almost persuasive. The most famous version of the argument is found in the *Proslogion* of St. Anselm of Canterbury (1033-1109), who, like Augustine, was a Christian neoplatonist. Another version is found in Descartes' *Meditations on First Philosophy*.

Augustine's ontological argument, found in *On Free Choice of the Will*, starts out a lot like Anselm's. Both men quote Psalm 14:1 "The fool has said in his heart, 'There is no God,'" and both appeal to the great chain of being. Moreover, both offer interesting, negative definitions of God as "that than which none greater can be conceived." Anselm, however, standing on Augustine's shoulders, has the more systematic presentation of the argument and comes closer to proving that what the fool has said must be false.

Augustine summarizes his own proof as follows:

> Now you had conceded that if I proved the existence of something higher than our minds, you would admit that it was God, as long as there was nothing higher still. I accepted this concession, and said that it would be enough if I proved that there is something higher than our minds. For if there is something more excellent than the truth, then that is God; if not, the truth itself is God. So in either case you cannot deny that God exists. [H 58]

As is evident, Augustine leaves the reader to fill in some of the steps.

Using further comments Augustine makes, we can capture the structure of his logic as follows:

1. If we can find something superior to the mind, then we have proven that God exists, for either that thing is God (that than which none greater can be conceived), or there is something greater than what we have found, and that will be God.
2. If there is something that the mind seeks, then it must be superior to the mind.
3. The mind seeks truth.
4. Truth is superior the mind.
5. Truth exists.
6. Therefore, either truth is God, or if there is something superior to truth, then *that* is God.
7. Therefore, God exists.

If this is Augustine's argument, it is not very persuasive because too many of the premises assert things that the fool is unlikely to accept.

Anselm's version of the proof is a bit more persuasive. He argues that the fool, if he understands the language, must admit that he has an idea of God, as that than which nothing is superior. Next, Anselm makes the claim that what exists as an idea *and* in reality is superior to that which exists only as an idea. Thus, to think of God as not existing in reality is not to be thinking of God as he is defined; if the fool is thinking about God as defined, he *must* be thinking of a being that actually exists.

41

The standard objection to the ontological argument works against both Anselm and Augustine. It was first advanced by Gaunilo of Marmoutier, who was a contemporary of Anselm. Gaunilo shows that one cannot prove that something exists by simply defining it as "that than which none greater can be conceived." He asks us to imagine the "Island of the blessed," an island than which none greater can be conceived. Obviously, if this island lived up to its definition, it would have to exist in reality and not just as an idea. It does not, however, exist in reality.

Even though some contemporary philosophers are still committed to a version of the ontological argument (see, for example, Alvin Plantinga, *The Ontological Argument: From St. Anselm to Contemporary Philosophers*, Anchor Books, 1965), most philosophers reject it. Augustine's innatism stands or falls with the existence of God. The fact that the ontological argument cannot prove the existence of God, however, does not prove that it falls. Divine illumination theory may still be true. Whether it is or not, it has made an important contribution to intellectual history.

3.7 Augustine's Contribution to Science

Despite his rejection of empiricism, Augustine did not reject the external world. Most neoplatonists regarded the body and all of nature as a detestable prison. Augustine, in contrast, is deeply interested in these things, and praises their beauty. He admires the human body so much that he denies the popular neoplatonic thesis that the afterlife is lived in a disembodied state. He insists, on the contrary, that God will rejuvenate each of our bodies and give them back to us in heaven. [See C 1052ff.] Augustine also admires nature. His writings are riddled with passages describing the glory of creation with hymnlike enthusiasm.

Augustine's appreciation of the natural world made him an acute observer. Throughout his works he puzzles over the curiosities of nature more than most writers of his day. How is it that, when you cut a centipede in half, both halves live on as though nothing happened? Why can some people wiggle their ears and others not? Questions such as these fascinated Augustine.

Augustine was not a scientist. In fact, later in his life he would become very suspicious and disdainful of scientific progress. Nevertheless, in his early works, he thinks about the natural world in a way that would be useful in stimulating future scientific thought.

An episode in Book Seven of *Confessions* illustrates this. As a youth, Augustine was intrigued with astrology. The more he thought about it, however, the more skeptical he became. He generated what we would now call a thought experiment concerning the Biblical twins Jacob and Esau in order to test the astrologer's claim. He writes,

> I set myself to consider the case of those who are born twins, who usually emerge from the womb so close to each other that the small interval of time involved—however much influence they claim that it has in nature—cannot be estimated by any human observation so as to be set down in the tables which the astrologer has to inspect in order to pronounce the truth. It will not be the truth. For instance anyone inspecting those tables would have had to foretell the same future for Esau and Jacob, but the same things did not happen to them. Therefore he would either have had to foretell falsely, or else if he foretold truly then he would have had to see different things in the same horoscope. So again we see that any truth he spoke would have been by chance not skill. [D 114]

This crisp little argument, which hardly needs commentary, is still effective today as a refutation of one of the more tenacious examples of pseudoscience. One of the fathers of modern science, Sir Francis Bacon (1561-1626), would recognize it as an example of a "cruxial experiment," or an "instance of the fingerpost." And Sir Karl Popper (1902-94) would see in it a foreshadowing of his own criteria for demarcating science from pseudoscience: falsifiability and the ability to make risky predictions

Augustine's most important overall contribution to science, however, lies in his attitude toward truth. Critics regard the theological component of his epistemology as a handicap. Nevertheless, it is this same theological component that inspires Augustine's staunch commitment to objectivism.

There are two main ways of thinking about truth. Objectivists think of a true statement as a report of a single reality that is independent of the mind and ultimately the same for everyone. If someone points to a stone and says, "This is a stone," then what he says is true even if someone else does not experience the object as a stone. If someone else does not experience the object as a stone, then the object must be tested until it can be determined who is right. Subjectivists, in contrast, think of a true statement as an opinion about the way the world seems to the person making the statement. On the subjectivist view, it can be true to one person that the object is a stone, while at the same time, true to someone else that it is not a stone. There is no test that can determine the matter for everyone once and for all. Objectivism and subjectivism are two fundamentally opposed ways of looking at the world.

Various versions of subjectivism are popular in certain philosophical circles today. And subjectivism is not new. The Pyrrhonian skepticism of Carneades, for example, amounts to a version of it. It is safe to say, however, that the overwhelming majority of scientists throughout history have been objectivists of one stripe or another. If we had always accepted everyone's opinions as equally valid, we would never have discovered that the earth is not in the center of the cosmos. Nonetheless, it is difficult to maintain objectivism in a world full of misleading appearances.

Augustine believed that God is the reality beyond the appearances. Not only is he the *source* of truth, in the form of divine illumination, he *is* the truth. Therefore Augustine's deep devotion to God immediately translates into a deep devotion to objectivism.

In some places, Augustine describes truth with an intensity that is frankly erotic. In *Soliloquies*, for example, he writes,

> Now, we are trying to discover what kind of a lover of wisdom you are: that wisdom which you desire to behold and to possess with purest gaze and embrace, with no veil between and, as it were, naked: such as wisdom allows to very few and these the most chosen of its lovers. If you were inflamed with the love of some beautiful woman, would she not rightly refuse to give herself to you if she discovered that you loved anything but herself? And will the purest beauty of wisdom reveal itself to you unless you burn for it alone?
> [L, I, 372-3]

Elsewhere, he presents a more muted, but still uncompromising objectivism:

> We make these judgements *in accordance* with the inner rules of truth, which we perceive n common; but no one makes judgements *about* those rules. When someone says that eternal things are better than temporal things, or that seven plus three equals ten, no one says that it ought to be so. We simply recognize that it is so; we are like explorers who rejoice in what they have discovered, not like inspectors who have to put things right. [H 54]

Augustine's reverence for truth, and his claim that we could attain truth even when the prospects for success looked discouraging, helped to shape the course of intellectual history throughout the Middle Ages and beyond.

4

The Inner Man

Augustine is often credited with inventing the "inner man." We can understand this claim on two levels. First, we can understand it on the level of style. Augustine so often writes from his own experience and reveals deeply personal facts about himself along the way—the kinds of facts that no other author before him had ever dared to reveal. Second, we can understand it on a philosophical level in connection with his unprecedented use of the concept of memory. We have already seen that Augustine agrees with the innatist thesis that knowledge is remembered rather than acquired. He goes further than most innatists do, however, in exploring the concept of memory and using it to address a number of difficult philosophical issues.

4.1 The Trinity

Sometimes philosophical ideas come from the strangest of places. Augustine's conception of memory emerged from his meditations on the doctrine of the trinity. It is necessary to understand this theological context in order to understand why memory becomes such a pivotal concept in his philosophy of mind.

The doctrine of the Trinity holds that, although there is one God, God has three persons: the Father, the Son, and the Holy Spirit. This is a difficult theological doctrine that is by no means clearly spelled out in the Bible. Christians debated for years over the question of how these three persons are supposed to be related. The debate was finally silenced at the council of Nicea in 381. The council of Nicea decreed that Christians should conceive of God neither as three nor as one but as Three-in-One.

Although the council of Nicea silenced the debate, it did not settle the issue. What does it mean to say that something is three-in-one? Augustine was a new convert to Christianity in 386, and he found himself puzzling over this question. The Christian Church desperately needed a theologian who could explain the doctrine in a satisfying way. This was a task that lay waiting for Augustine when he became bishop in 396.

Although Augustine felt overwhelmed by the task, somewhere along the line, a clever idea occurred to him. The Bible states that human beings are made in the image of God. We want to understand God, but have no direct access to him. So, why not study the image instead? Suddenly, it dawned on Augustine that the human soul is a trinity. He thought that by studying the trinity in the human soul he could better understand the trinity of God. By Book Thirteen of *Confessions*, the idea was in its infancy. Augustine writes,

> It would be good if men would meditate upon three things to be found in themselves. . . . The three things of which I speak are existence, knowledge, will. For I am, and I know, and I will. I am a being that knows and wills: I know that I am and that I will: I will to be and to know. In these three there is inseparable life, one life, one mind, one essence: so that it is impossible to effect separation: yet the three are distinct. Let him see this who can. At any rate the fact is within himself; let him look attentively at himself and see and tell me. [D 266-7]

Augustine speculates that these three aspects of the soul, existence, knowledge, and will, are analogous to the three persons of God: the Father, the Son, and the Holy Spirit.

The idea soon matured into an entire book called *On the Trinity*. The first half of the book is a vast mire of Biblical exegesis and hardcore theology. In the second half, Augustine applies the model of the trinity to his philosophy of mind.

The entire project is a bit disappointing from a strictly philosophical point of view. Augustine's trinitarian explanation of the mind at times seems more a desperate attempt to lend some plausibility to Christian dogma than a careful investigation of a very difficult philosophical area. To the unsympathetic reader, it is a convoluted way of going about things.

Nevertheless, it was in meditating upon the mind as a trinity that Augustine began to develop a fruitful analysis of memory. In *Confessions*, he characterized the three aspects of the soul as existence, knowledge, and will. In *On the Trinity*, these categories shift slightly to become memory, understanding, and love. Love (or will) is analogous to the Holy Spirit because the role of the Holy Spirit is to unite human beings. Understanding (or knowledge) is analogous to the Son because the role of the Son is to make truth manifest to men. But why is memory analogous to the Father? The role of the Father is to create and sustain existence. What is it that plays this role at the level of the human soul? Augustine's answer is memory. Our very existence as human beings springs from and feeds on memory.

It would be too much to canvass all the different ways that Augustine makes his case for the centrality of memory in human existence. In what follows, we will look at the three most seminal suggestions he makes.

4.2 The Subconscious

The first suggestion is just a very small seed that would take many centuries to flower and bear fruit.

One aspect of the mind that contemporary philosophers find inexplicable, while at the same time undeniable, is the subconscious. The subconscious encompasses a range of mental activity that human beings engage in while completely unaware. Consider the woman who each day swears that she has never regretted not having children, and each night dreams that she is a mother. Some people would say that, deep inside, she knows that she has made the wrong choice. Yet, for some reason, her conscious mind refuses to acknowledge this. One could imagine catching this same woman window shopping at toy stores. If you ask her why she is there, she will give a perfectly reasonable-sounding excuse that has nothing to do with her secret motherhood fantasy. The subconscious is puzzling because the mind seems to know something while at the same time not knowing that it knows.

The most famous theorist of the subconscious was, of course, the psychologist Sigmund Freud (1856-1939). Freud believed that everyone has secret fantasies, and that they are often surprisingly sexual or violent in nature. In his view, many of the dramatic themes found in classic literature are actually common subconscious desires that no one dares admit to. In the Greek play, *Oedipus Rex*, the hero of the story unknowingly kills his father and marries his mother. Freud hypothesized that many men, deep inside, have violent feelings toward their fathers and sexual feelings toward their mothers. He called it the "oedipal complex." In healthy individuals, the mind is strong enough to keep such subconscious desires suppressed. If it is not strong enough, however, individuals become neurotic, and begin to exhibit anti-social behavior. Freud developed the technique of psychoanalysis to help such individuals regain mental balance.

The connection between Freud and Augustine is unmistakable.

First of all, both relied on Plato for ideas about the divided structure of the mind.

Second, Augustine was himself a textbook case of the oedipal complex. His relations with his father were strained. It is striking that Augustine, who so eloquently mourns death, even of people whom he has never met, only barely mentions his father's death in passing. Meanwhile, his relations with his mother were stifling. Freudian readers of *Confessions* have made much of the passage in which Augustine divulges that Monica had a "too earthly affection" for him. [D 77]

Finally, and most importantly, Augustine discovers the subconscious in *On the Trinity*. He writes,

> This tells us that in the recesses of the mind there are various awarenesses of various things, and that they come out somehow into the open and are set as it were more clearly in the mind's view when they are thought about; it is then that the mind discovers it remembers and understands and loves something too, which it was not thinking about while it was thinking about something else. But if it is something that we have not thought about for a long time and are unable to think about unless we are reminded of it, then in heaven knows what curious way it is something, if you can say this, that we do not know we know. At least it is quite correct for the man who is doing the reminding to say to the man he reminds, "You know this, but you do not know that you know it; I will remind you, and you will discover that you know what you supposed you did not know." Literature performs precisely this function, when it is about things that the reader discovers under the guidance of reason to be true, not simply believing the writer that they are true as when he reads history, but himself discovering with the writer that they are true, and discovering it either in himself or in truth itself guiding the mind. But anyone who is unable to see these things even when he is reminded of them and has his attention drawn to them, is suffering from a great blindness of heart and sunk very deep in the darkness of ignorance, and needs very special aid from God to be able to attain true wisdom. [K, I/5, 377]

If Augustine had been an atheist, like Freud, he may well have invented psychoanalysis. Short of that, he calls on God, and thinks of the subconscious as just another facet of human memory.

It is worth noting that not many thinkers between Augustine and Freud picked up on the idea of the subconscious. Even Descartes, despite his innatism, stubbornly maintains that the activity of the mind is transparent to itself.

4.3 Mental Language

Another area in which Augustine vindicates the centrality of memory is in philosophy of language. Augustine's philosophy of language is simple, yet powerful and compelling. It was powerful and compelling enough to attract the attention of the most famous recent philosopher of language, Ludwig Wittgenstein (1889-1951). In *Philosophical Investigations*, Wittgenstein quotes Augustine twice. This is noteworthy because *Philosophical Investigations* is a work in which references to other philosophers are sparing, while actual quotations are almost non-existent.

Here is the quotation that opens *Philosophical Investigations*, from Book One of *Confessions*:

> [I observed that] my elders would make some particular sound, and as they made it would point at or move towards some particular thing: and from this I came to realize that the thing was called by the sound they made when they wished to draw my attention to it. That they intended this was clear from the motions of their body, by a kind of natural language common to all races which consists of facial expressions, glances of the eye, gestures, and the tones by which the voice expresses the mind's state—for example whether things are to be sought, kept, thrown away, or avoided. So, as I heard the same words again and again properly used in different phrases, I came gradually to grasp what things they signified; and forcing my mouth to the same sounds, I began to use them to express my own wishes. [D 9]

In this passage, Augustine presents the notion of ostensive definition—establishing the meaning of a word by pointing.

Augustine's philosophy of language relies heavily on the notion of ostensive definition. In his view, words refer to objects in the world. This is to say that words are symbols that are only meaningful insofar as they are understood to stand for something that exists independently of them. Linguistic activity relies on a direct correspondence between the realm of words or signs and the realm of things.

This theory seems plausible enough. It is certainly easy to think of examples to support it. We use flash cards and picture books to teach children how to speak, read, and write. It seems that the use of ostensive definition is crucial to language acquisition.

Wittgenstein, however, rejects Augustine's theory. He argues instead that linguistic activity is a "form of life" analogous to playing a game. What is important is that people know how to make the right moves. The activity is self-contained. It does not refer to something outside of itself. In Wittgenstein's view, the meaning of a word comes, not from its referent, but from its being used in a particular way.

This is a provocative suggestion. In order to be a competent speaker of English, you need to know which uses of the word "pig" are appropriate, and which are not. We can imagine human beings carrying on elaborate conversations about pigs even if there never was any such thing as a pig to point to. Many people hold, in fact, that this is exactly what has happened in the case of God. Religious language is a form of life that refers to nothing beyond itself. Perhaps the same is ultimately true of all words. After all, according to certain anti-realist or subjectivist views, it is not entirely clear whether things like stones and pigs really exist, or, if they do, what they really are. Nevertheless we all know how to talk about them. If our linguistic activity is nothing but a self-contained game, then ostensive definition is just another move in the game, it does not refer beyond the game itself.

In *Philosophical Investigations* [§32], Wittgenstein attempts to refute Augustine's referential view on the grounds that one would need to know a language already in order to learn language in the way Augustine describes.

We can understand Wittgenstein's point as follows. Suppose the empiricist is right, and human beings are born as perfectly blank slates. Imagine, under these circumstances, trying to teach some children the word "walk." You point to someone who is walking and say "walk." How are the children supposed to know that, by pointing your finger, you mean to indicate something beyond your finger? In order to follow you, the children would already have to have something in mind, a concept (the concept of walking), that needed a name.

For Wittgenstein, this proves that the referential theory of language fails. In his view, we do not already have concepts in mind when we learn language. Therefore, we cannot learn a language by associating a word with this concept. Wittgenstein suggests that one might use ostensive definition in order to learn a *second* language. If you already know the word "*ambulare*," then you can learn the English word "walk" by associating it with the Latin word that you already have in mind. This will not work, however, as a general theory of language acquisition, according to Wittgenstein.

Augustine can defend himself against Wittgenstein's critique much more readily than most people realize.

First of all, he is quite clear that ostensive definition relies on attention to tone and facial expression that comprises "a kind of natural language common to all races." [D 9] This sort of holism will not go as far as Wittgenstein's "forms of life," but the theory is not as poverty stricken as some critics make out.

Secondly, Augustine denies the empiricist thesis that human beings are born blank slates. Human beings are born with minds that are fully stocked with a supply of innate ideas. Augustine uses the example of happiness. Each child has a concept of happiness in the mind that needs a name.

Finally, Augustine acknowledges that ostensive definition amounts to learning a second language in so far as he posits that the human mind comes built with a first language, a mental language, consisting in the inner words of thought. He hints at this in many places but it becomes most clear during his discussion of memory in Book Nine of *On the Trinity*. Augustine writes,

> And by this form we conceive true knowledge of things, which we have with us as a kind of word that we beget by uttering inwardly, and that does not depart from us when it is born. When we speak to others we put our voice or some bodily gesture at the disposal of the word that abides within, in order that by a kind of perceptible reminder the same sort of thing might happen in the mind of the listener as exists in and does not depart from the mind of the speaker. And so there is nothing that we do with our bodies in deeds or words to express approval or disapproval of the behavior of men, which we have not anticipated with a word uttered inside ourselves. Nobody voluntarily does anything that he has not previously uttered as a word in his heart. [K, I/5, 277-8]

The words of the inner man form a basis for understanding and interacting with the world.

It may not be going too far to claim that Augustine is suggesting that, despite differences between various spoken languages, and despite differences in what is now called "surface grammar," there may be a "deep grammar" common to all human beings. If this is correct, Augustine can be seen as laying some very tentative groundwork for the innatist theory of language that can be traced through William of Ockham (1285-1349) and is today associated with Noam Chomsky

(1928-). Innatist language theorists hold that learning a language is a matter of learning to associate spoken and written words with internal words. These internal words form a language, common to all human beings, sometimes called "mentalese."

4.4 Time

In addition to the subconscious and mental language, Augustine also uses the concept of memory to develop a distinctive theory of time. It is found primarily in Book Eleven of *Confessions* and in Book Nine of *City of God*.

Augustine's investigation of time is motivated, first of all, by his desire to understand the opening phrase of the book of Genesis: "In the beginning..." If God is eternal, and therefore had no beginning, then what can "in the beginning" mean for him? Furthermore, what was God doing before creation?

These questions become particularly acute when one is presented with the cosmological argument for the existence of God. The cosmological argument claims that the principle of prior causation shows that there must be a cause of the world that is prior to it in time, and that this cause must be God.

The problem with the argument is that it is not clear why the principle of prior causation does not apply to God as well. Why is it not necessary that there be a cause of God that is prior to him in time? Defenders of the argument reply that God is uncaused. Only God can be an exception to the principle of prior causation because only he exists eternally. Unfortunately, this only raises a further question: if the principle of prior causation admits of an exception, why not let the world itself be the uncaused eternal thing rather than God?

The cosmological argument was most famously stated long after Augustine by Thomas Aquinas (1224-74). Nevertheless, the core idea of the argument and the underlying cosmological questions are at least as old as Aristotle and would have been transmitted to Augustine through neoplatonist thinkers.

Augustine's other motivation for the study of time stems just from the sheer mystery surrounding the concept. Consider the paradox mentioned in the novel, *The Flanders Panel* by the Spanish author Arturo Pérez-Reverte (translated by Margaret J. Costa, Bantam Books, 1996):

"The sentence I am now writing is the sentence you are now reading." [170]

How should you understand the word "now" in this sentence? To what does it refer? According to Augustine's theory of language, it must refer to something, and either this thing spans some time or it does not. If it does span some time, then there are times when not all of the now is now. If it does not span any time, then it does not exist. But then "now," since it has no referent, has no meaning.

Augustine was not above admitting that he was completely stumped by such paradoxes. This led him to write his most famous line, one that has been quoted many times throughout the history of philosophy: "What *is* this time? If no one asks me, I know; if I want to explain it to a questioner, I do not know." [D 219]

Despite his bafflement, Augustine attempts to answer the question of what God was doing before creation. His sense of humor allows him to consider and reject one answer: "He was getting Hell ready for people who pry too deep." [D 218] His own solution is to question the validity of the question. Time is the measure of motion. Before creation, there was no motion; therefore, before creation, there was no time. If there was no time before creation, then the question, "What was God doing before creation?" is incoherent. There was no *before* in which God can be seen as acting. God does not live in time but in eternity, which is a form of duration that does not involve change.

This way of answering the question commits Augustine to the thesis that time is not a necessary feature of reality, but rather a contingent feature of creation. In order to understand how Augustine makes sense of this thesis, we need to examine his position in some detail.

There are two broad stances one might adopt regarding the nature of time, namely, realism and anti-realism.

Realists assert that time has an objective, external existence. This existence is independent of actual perception of time by the human mind. The classic example of a realist is Sir Isaac Newton (1642-1727), who conceived of space and time as a multidimensional container in which all of reality is situated. Other realists include Plato and Albert Einstein (1879-1955). In Plato's creation myth *Timeus*, we find the following famous passage:

> He (the creator) thought of making a certain movable image of eternity, and, at once with ordering heaven, he made an eternal image going according to number, that which we have named Time [37d6, quoted in M 4]

And here is Einstein:

> It might appear possible to overcome all difficulties attending the definition of "time" by substituting "the position of the small hand of my watch" for "time." [M 7]

The only significant difference between these two views is that, for Plato, time is absolute (the same everywhere), and is measured by the motion of the celestial bodies, while for Einstein, time is relative to the perceiver, and its measurement is local.

Augustine makes short work of realism. Against the Platonic view, he points out [D 225-26] that we would still measure time if the celestial motions were to speed up, slow down, or cease. In fact, how would we register changes in celestial motion unless through an internal sense of time? Against Einstein, we can imagine Augustine arguing that we would still sensibly measure the passage of time even if all of our clocks were broken. And of course, Augustine has scriptural support for his view. After all, Joshua stops the sun in time.

Augustine derives his anti-realism from an analysis of the three "parts" of time: past, present, and future. He writes,

> But the two times, past and future, how can they *be*, since the past is no more and the future is not yet? On the other hand, if the present were always present and never flowed away into the past, it would not be time at all, but eternity. But if the present is the only time, because it flows away into the past, how can we say that it *is*? For it is, only because it will cease to be. Thus we can affirm that time *is* only in that it tends towards not-being. [D 219]

Augustine reasons that it should be a requirement of any existing thing that its proper parts exist. The proper parts of time are the past, the present, and the future. But none of these is an existing thing. Time, therefore, is not an existing thing.

In support of his anti-realism, Augustine offers an argument for the claim that the present can have no duration. It seems like it does have duration in so far as we often say things like, "It is now the twenty-first century." Augustine asks, however, whether the present could refer to a hundred-year stretch of time. This would be impossible, since in the first of the hundred years, the other 99 would still be in the future. If this argument is iterated to consider presents that have durations of a year, a month, a day, an hour, or a second, then the same conclusion will follow. Thus, the future does not yet exist, the past has ceased to be, and even the now has only an evanescent reality.

By denying that time has an objective, external existence, however, Augustine does not thereby deny the reality of time, as do Buddhists, for example, or philosophers like J.M.E. McTaggart (1866-1925). Augustine is an internalist. For him, time is a feature of the inner man: it is the soul measuring motion and change. Although time does not exist outside the mind, it does exist within the mind as memories or expectations. One's memory of one's childhood exists now, as does one's expectation of tomorrow's rising sun. Augustine writes,

> At any rate it is now quite clear that neither future nor past actually exists. Nor is it right to say there are three times, past, present, and future. Perhaps it would be more correct to say: there are three times, a present of things past, a present of things present, a present of things future, for these three things exist in the mind, and I find them nowhere else: the present of things past is memory, the present of things present is sight, the present of things future is expectation. [D 223]

Although it follows from this view that no time enjoys objective external existence, Augustine makes it clear that he has no objection to our following custom and continuing to speak of past, present, and future.

Augustine asserts that time is nothing but the soul measuring motion and change. He cannot deny, however, that we also measure time itself. What, then, are we measuring? Augustine comes to this problem in §§26 and 27 of Book Eleven of *Confessions*. There he declares that the mind measures time by measuring and illuminating memories and expectations that exist in the present and have extension. Having failed to find any mind-independent measure of time, he says that time is a kind of "extendedness" of the mind itself. He writes,

> It is in you, O my mind, that I measure time. ... What I measure is the impress produced in you by things as they pass and abiding in you when they have passed: and it is present. I do not measure the things themselves whose passage produced the impress; it is the impress that I measure when I measure time. Thus either that is what time is, or I am not measuring time at all. . . . But how is the future diminished or exhausted, since the future does not yet exist: or how does the past grow, since it no longer is? Only because, in the mind which does all this, there are three acts. For the mind expects, attends and remembers. ... Would anyone deny that the future is as yet not existent? But in the mind there is already an expectation of the future. ... Thus it is not the future that is long, for the future does not exist: a long future is merely a long expectation of the future. [D 229-30]

Augustine's argument hinges on the metaphor of the extendedness or "stretching" of the mind.

What is the stretching of the mind? It is evident that Augustine regards this activity as one that will bring us closer to (an understanding of) God. The durationless "now" from which the mind extends itself to

55

consider the past and the future may be the intersection between our temporal existence and the eternal, atemporal existence of God. Augustine suggests that a mind that is able to stretch itself enough to illuminate all of the past and the future would have a knowledge of all time. This would not be knowledge of eternity, but it would be as close as a human being could come to God.

Despite its mystical leanings, Augustine's theory continues to attract serious attention. Perhaps the most famous example is *On the Phenomenology of Internal Time Consciousness*, by the German phenomenologist Edmund Husserl (1859-1938). In this book, Husserl not only recommends Book Nine of *Confessions* as mandatory reading on the problem of time, he also proudly presents himself as carrying on the Augustinian internalist tradition. The American psychologist and philosopher, William James (1842-1910) is another internalist. (A reader interested in a comparative study should consult Eva Brann's *What, Then, is Time?*, Rowman and Littlefield, 1999. This book contains a comparative discussion of Augustine and Husserl, and covers many other major theorists about time, including Plato, Aristotle, Plotinus, Newton, Leibniz, Kant, Hegel, Bergson, Einstein, and Heidegger.)

One criticism of Augustine's account is that it is circular. Augustine asserts that time is nothing but thought and then goes on to assert that thought can be short or long. How are we to measure the length of a thought if not with time? Either Augustine is using the idea of time passing to explain time, in which case his explanation is circular, or he will need some other measure for thought, in which case we will soon be enmeshed in an in an infinite regress. This dilemma arises because of the problem of the criterion, which Augustine put to such good use in his refutation of the Academic skeptics. Ironically, it has now come back to plague his own theory of time.

Another sort of criticism comes in slightly different forms from Immanuel Kant and from Wittgenstein. Both would argue that Augustine is asking a question that cannot be answered in the way that he thinks it has to be answered.

Kant's view of the nature of time does not easily lend itself to brief treatment. What we can say, however, is that, in the section of his *Critique of Pure Reason* called "The Antinomy of Pure Reason," Kant argues that when we try to reason about such concepts as eternity or the beginning of time (or God, for that matter), we become confused, and the confusion is incurable. Augustine's mistake was in trying to reason about time as he would about ordinary material concepts.

The contemporary philosopher Richard Gale (1932-) presents a related concern. In his introduction to *The Philosophy of Time*, Gale points out that no one has ever asked, "What *is* yellow?" The reason for this is that it is easy to provide an ostensive definition of yellow. If, for some reason, we were unable to point out instances of yellow, it would be almost impossible to convey what the word "yellow" means. (The answer to the effect that yellow is light at wavelengths between 575 and 585 nanometers does not count, as it will not help someone who does not know what yellow looks like.) The problem with time is that we cannot provide an ostensive definition. The things we can point to, such the celestial movements and clocks, do not constitute time itself. Time itself is not something you can point to. Hence, if we are going to find a definition of time, it seems it will have to be a non-ostensive definition. The difficulty with formulating a non-ostensive definition, even of familiar, well understood concepts might have led Augustine to question the prospects for his inquiry concerning time.

Of course, Augustine identifies time with memory and expectation precisely because he refuses to give up the search for an ostensive definition of time. This is ironic considering that, in his theodicy, the word "evil" does not refer to any properly existing thing.

Wittgenstein would agree with Kant and Gale that Augustine has been misled by his philosophy of language and by the grammatical similarity between "What *is* time?" and "What is a fruit? We think that these are questions to be answered in the same way, but they are not. For Wittgenstein, it is enough that we know how to use the word and the concept in question. Augustine clearly admits that he knows how to use the concept of time and its relatives. Any further questioning, according to Wittgenstein, is just a confusion about grammar [*Philosophical Investigations*, §§89-90], or "language idling." Augustine's mistake was to try to apply language relevant for measuring spatial relationships to the measurement of time. Wittgenstein accuses Augustine of forgetting that words can be ambiguous and equivocal. [*The Blue Book* §§26-27]

Thus, Wittgenstein would have us dissolve Augustine's question instead of solving it. This dissolution is a kind of therapy supplied by paying attention to grammar. The problem with Wittgenstein's approach, which Kant would have foreseen, is that the puzzlement will not go away. Augustine was right to be troubled by the nature of time and the problems that arise when we try to think about it. His attempts at solutions, while problematic, should not be dismissed as futile.

5
Ethics and Political Theory

Political theorists fall into two main categories. Political optimists believe that a good government can improve the human condition; political pessimists deny that any government can have a positive impact on human beings. In modern times, Americans Thomas Jefferson (1743-1826) and John Rawls (1921-) are examples of optimists, while anarchists and extreme libertarians are political pessimists.

Plato and Aristotle are examples of political optimists in the ancient world. In his *Republic*, Plato argues that human beings can achieve justice by organizing society in a hierarchical fashion. He describes this hierarchy in detail and explains why he thinks it will improve the human condition. In his *Politics*, Aristotle criticizes various theories, including Plato's, and presents his vision of the ideal society. He argues that justice can be achieved through democracy. Both Plato and Aristotle served as advisors to real politicians during their careers. They believed that politics could make an important difference in life on Earth.

Augustine, in contrast, is a political pessimist. He never bothers to develop an argument for one ideal form of government as opposed to another because he is convinced that all are equally worthless. To this extent, Augustine does not make much of a constructive contribution to political theory.

Augustine does, however, develop an extensive argument for political pessimism itself. One might say he develops a "metatheory" designed to show the proper place of politics in the cosmos. This metatheory, heavily dependent on his ethical theory, was deeply influential in shaping Western history.

5.1 City of God, City of Man

Augustine's approach to politics was strongly influenced by his experiences living in the Roman Empire during the final days of its decline and fall. The Christian Church, which had started out as a small counter-culture movement, was gaining power every day. Meanwhile, the state was slowly falling apart. The people of the Roman Empire were in the habit of calling Rome the "Eternal City." It was enormous and magnificent. No one wanted to believe it was on the verge of collapse.

One of the main difficulties was religious strife. There were vast numbers of Christians and pagans living together in the Roman Empire and they were at odds. During the first three centuries after Christ, the pagans had control of the government. They saw the Christians as a threat, and regularly persecuted them. They were far from successful, however, in making Christianity disappear. After Emperor Constantine converted to Catholicism, Christianity gained the upper hand. By 394, pagan worship had been outlawed. Continued hostility between pagans and Christians, however, undermined the daily business of the Empire and weakened it.

Barbarians sacked Rome for the first time in 410. News of the atrocities they visited upon the "Eternal City" sent shock waves throughout the empire. Pagans saw this as the final blow in the recent string of assaults against their gods. They blamed the Christians. Most Christians, on the other hand, had hoped that they were moving into a golden age. They were asking, "Why would God allow this to happen now?"

Augustine wrote the massive treatise *City of God* as a response to the sack of Rome. He wanted to show why the fall of the Roman Empire was not the Christians' fault and to argue that the destruction of Rome was part of God's plan all along. The central thesis of the book is that God reveals his justice through the trials and tribulations of human history.

What has God revealed through the destruction of Rome? That human beings should not put their faith in things of this world. Christians were wrong to see the conversion of the Empire as a triumph. One cannot accomplish spiritual goals through politics.

Augustine was in a good position to make this argument because, as a bishop, he had been dealing first hand with the effects of the alliance between Rome and Christianity. Once a religion becomes official there arises the problem of false conversion—people who go through the motions of conversion to avoid persecution or to enjoy the benefits of the official religion. Augustine learned that false conversion can be far worse than no conversion at all.

It was not just the falsely converted pagans but also the falsely converted Donatists that worried Augustine. The Donatists, named after their fourth century North African founder Donatus, were a large schismatic Christian sect. Unlike the Manichees and the Pelagians, the Donatists did not have any major doctrinal disputes with Catholicism. Rather, they were purists—they simply wanted Catholics to live up to their own ideals more stringently.

Donatism began in the days when the Roman Empire persecuted Christians. During purging periods, Catholic bishops and priests who refused to renounce their faith would often be tortured and killed. Although many of them held out, and became martyrs as a result, many also gave in under the pressure and renounced their faith. Then, when the purging period was over, they wanted to be readmitted to the church.

The Donatists did not want to readmit those who had let their faith lapse. They claimed that anyone who was baptized by one of the *lapsi* was not really baptized. They also staged various acts of violence against the *lapsi* and their defenders. Augustine, who was in favor of forgiving and readmitting the *lapsi*, was himself threatened and once nearly ambushed by angry Donatists. Augustine came to believe that Donatists were not true Christians because they spurned the Christian value of forgiveness.

In 405, Donatism was banned. Of course, banning heresy was nothing new: there had been heresies before, and they had been banned before. What made this ban different, however, is that it was enforced by the state. It was legal authority, not merely religious authority, which forced the Donatists to return to their churches.

As a result of imperial pressure against the pagans and the schismatic Christians alike, churches were increasingly populated by *ficti*—people who were not Catholic but claimed to be in order to avoid discrimination, fines, imprisonment, or worse. The alliance of church and state had resulted in an obvious dilution of Catholicism.

Who were the true believers? Augustine looked out into the faces in his swelling congregation and saw a mixed bag. He knew a few of them were true believers and a lot of them were not; he also knew he could never be sure exactly which ones were which.

This situation—living in a world that on the surface contained only Catholics but at a deeper level was sharply divided—led Augustine to develop the famous concept that guides his political thought. The human race does not form a single, unified community. Rather, it is composed of two fundamentally different kinds of people: the true believers and the unbelievers.

Augustine crystallizes his concept in a vivid image. The true believers and the unbelievers form two invisible cities on Earth, each with its own destiny. Augustine writes,

> I classify the human race into two branches: the one consists of those who live by human standards, the other of those who live according to God's will. I also call these two classes the two cities, speaking allegorically. By "two cities" I mean two societies of human beings, one of which is predestined to reign with God for all eternity, the other doomed to undergo eternal punishment with the Devil. [C 595]

Human beings have one thing in common: none of us deserves to reign with God for all eternity. Nevertheless, because God has chosen some of us for this destiny and others not, we are permanently divided. Some of us inhabit the City of God, and some the City of Man.

Rome symbolizes the City of Man, which Augustine also calls the "earthly city." He writes,

> The earthly city will not be everlasting; for when it is condemned to the final punishment it will no longer be a city. It has its good in this world, and rejoices to participate in it with such gladness as can be derived from things of such a kind. And since this is not the kind of good that causes no frustrations to those enamoured of it, the earthly city is generally divided against itself by litigation, by wars, by battles, by the pursuit of victories that bring death with them or at best are doomed to death. [C 599]

By "City of Man" Augustine does not literally mean Rome, or any other actual city. Rather, he is referring metaphorically to the discontented state of mind, the corrupted existence, of all those who do not truly believe in God.

The Catholic Church symbolizes the City of God. It cannot be fully realized in this world, but only in heaven. Augustine writes,

> And here also that blessed City will find in itself a great blessing, in that no inferior will feel envy of his superior, any more than the other angels are envious of the archangel. No one will wish to be what it has not been granted him to be; and yet he will be bound in the closest bond of peaceful harmony with one to whom it has been granted; just as in the body the finger does not wish to be the eye,

since both members are included in the harmonious organization of the whole body. [C 1088]

Augustine asserts that this harmony is only imperfectly reflected in the Catholic Church and its hierarchy. By "City of God," he does not mean to refer to any actual institution, but rather to the contented state of mind of all those who truly believe in God.

It is impossible to sort the members of the City of God from the members of the City of Man because membership is not just a matter of choice. Recall from Chapter Two that, for Augustine, human beings are incapable of doing anything good by themselves. True belief is something good. Therefore, human beings cannot become true believers by themselves. Rather, God gives true belief to some human beings and not to others. Peace of mind is a sign of the gift, but it is not a guarantee. Not even Augustine could be sure whether he had been chosen. The division among human beings is supernatural, and there is nothing we can do about it. This position has less in common with post-Augustinian Catholic thought than it has with post-reformation Calvinism.

In *City of God*, Augustine emphasizes the supernatural side of the theory. What always set Augustine apart as a philosopher, however, was his refusal to adopt any theory that lacked psychological validity. We have seen his interest in human psychology operating on a number of occasions. We should therefore raise the question: on what basis does Augustine assert that there exist these two kinds of people?

5.2 *Caritas* and *Cupiditas*

Augustine developed the main idea behind his political thought early in his philosophical career. It is heavily dependent on the neoplatonic idea of the great chain of being.

As human beings, we find ourselves in the midst of a universe in which some things are better than we are, some things are equal, and some are worse. If we focus our attention on the things that are better than we are we become better, we improve our existence. If we focus our attention on the things that are equal or worse, we stagnate or degenerate into a lesser existence.

According to Augustine, these two ways of focussing attention are different kinds of love. The improving love he calls "*caritas*," from which we derive the word "charity." The corrosive love he calls "*cupiditas*," from which we derive the word "cupidity," meaning lust or greed. The good life for human beings involves avoiding cupidity and cultivating charity in its place.

In Augustine's view, the problem with loving things that fall equal or lower than you on the great chain of being is that they are fragile. This is to say that you are guaranteed to loose them in a matter of time, often as a result of unpredictable events beyond your control. Why does that matter? Because losing things you love causes misery and bad behavior. And the more these things matter to you, the more of your own being you invest in them, the greater the loss.

Augustine is surely right about the harmful dimension of Cupid's arrow. Consider the man who loses his wife and child. He becomes depressed. Depression causes him to neglect his other obligations as well as recreation. In turn he becomes irritable and inclined to blame others for his misfortune. In severe cases, he is likely to hurt himself or someone else.

It is not just the actual loss that causes problems, however. The *fear* of losing something you love can be even worse. Think of the person obsessed with the need to check the stove, windows, and doors repeatedly before leaving the house. This obsession comes from the fear of losing prized possessions. Or again, the widespread phenomenon of over-protectionism in parents illustrates the point.

Augustine thought that fragility explains the disfunctionality evident in so many human relationships. He himself had experienced the problem over and over again in his life. After all, he had lost his lover and experienced the untimely deaths of his dear mother, best friends, and son. He writes,

> For not only are we troubled and anxious because they may be afflicted by famine, war, disease, or captivity, fearing that in slavery they may suffer evils beyond our powers of imagination; there is the much more bitter fear, that their friendship be changed into treachery, malice and baseness. And when such things do happen (and the more numerous our friends, the more often they happen) and the news is brought to our ears, who, except one who has this experience, can be aware of the burning sorrow that ravages our hearts? [C 862]

Grief and betrayal, lurking behind every relationship, spoil the secure sense of contentedness everyone needs.

Given this situation, how can human beings ever hope to be happy in this world? There is only one way: forget about the fragile goods here on earth, and turn your attention toward the one eternal good in heaven. The only way to survive the present life is to live it in expectation of the next. It is interesting that the contentedness Augustine seeks seems quite similar to the Pyrrhonian skeptics' desired state of *ata-*

raxia. Theories of happiness, known as eudaimonism, from the Greek word for happiness, were very common in ancient thought.

Augustine's argument for this view is most clearly stated in an early work called *The Catholic and Manichean Ways of Life.* He writes,

> For if happiness is the possession of a good than which there is no greater, and this is what we call the supreme good, how can people be said to be happy who have not yet attained their supreme good? Or how can it be called the supreme good if there is something better that they can attain? Such being the case, it follows that they cannot lose it against their will, for no one can be confident of a good they know can be snatched from them even though they wish to keep and cherish it. And if they lack this confidence in the good which they enjoy how can they, in such fear of loss, be happy? [B 6-7]

The line of reasoning underlying all of these rhetorical questions is quite simple. Happiness requires the best, the best includes confidence, and fragility undermines confidence. Therefore, happiness cannot be found in fragile goods.

Augustine's argument revolves around the psychological importance of confidence or reliability. If there are two equal goods, one of which is fragile and the other reliable, it would be irrational to prefer the fragile one. Moreover, even if the fragile good were to be, other things being equal, *better* than the reliable one, it would still be irrational to prefer the fragile one. For Augustine, fragility destroys peace of mind and therefore completely spoils a good thing.

Augustine's suggestion is not ridiculous. Imagine that you are buying stocks. You somehow find out that stock *A* is a sure win and that stock *B* is a sure loss. Even if you were, for whatever reason, attracted to stock *B*, you would be irrational not to opt for stock *A* instead. After all, stock *A* is a bird in the hand; stock *B* is ultimately nothing but pain and regret.

Blaise Pascal (1623-62), an avid reader of Augustine, turned this idea into his famous Wager. Every human being is faced with the choice of betting in favor of God or betting against God. If God exists, the advantages of the eternal reward you may gain if you bet on God by far outweigh any temporary reward you think you might gain by betting against God, particularly since only eternal damnation awaits those who wager incorrectly. And even if God does not exist, by wagering on the existence of God, one gains a kind of peace in this life, while wagering against leaves you in a world of fragile goods. Therefore, it is more rational to bet on God.

This is a powerful idea, although it is not without difficulties. Some critics have pointed out that it requires an extremely risk-averse conception of rationality. Consider the stock market example again. Why characterize stock *B* as a sure loss rather than a high risk? It does not seem obviously irrational to prefer a high risk with a large potential return to a more stodgy, safer stock. Augustine also owes the reader an explanation of why he supposes that God cannot be taken away from you against your will. God might decide to forsake you, as he forsook Esau. Being a maximally free being, he might do that to any one of us at any time.

One way to avoid this difficulty, a move that Augustine himself makes in several places, is to say that the object of human happiness is not precisely God but rather the love of God. Surely the love of God cannot be taken away from you against your will. This would be tantamount to saying that your will can change against your will, which seems like a contradiction.

Problems abound with this answer, however. First of all, it seems that some sort of brain damage could in fact change your love against your will. Suppose you go into a coma and become incapable of loving anything, much less God. Nor do we need such an extreme example. Suppose your subconscious is able to control your conscious beliefs and desires, as Augustine himself suggests. Secondly, if we interpret human happiness in terms of the possession of the love of an object rather than possession of the object itself, then a question arises as to why that object needs to be God. No one can take your love for your wife and child away from you. Even if they are killed, you can still love them with all your heart.

Perhaps Augustine would respond to these worries by pointing out that although love of God is not guaranteed to be reliable, it is the only thing that is not guaranteed to be fragile. Only God can make you last forever. Therefore only God can make you truly happy. He may not, but it is the only chance you have.

Augustine was looking for a theory of happiness. He observed an enormous difference between those who love fragile things and those who do not. It is the difference between being discontented and being content. These two states of mind are so different, in his view, that they carve the human race into separate societies.

This psychology provides some grounding for Augustine's political theory, but it also raises the question of ethics. Given that human beings are forced to live our lives on earth, we have to interact with fragile things. How should people who like to think of themselves as members of the City of God regard these things? This is the question that led to Augustine's highly controversial distinction between use and enjoyment.

5.3 Use and Enjoyment

So far we have seen Augustine's most basic psychological distinction between two kinds of love: cupidity and charity. Cupidity is bad, disordered love, love that is always wrong. Charity is good, well-ordered love, love that is always right. There is also a distinction to be made, however, between two kinds of charity.

First, there is the charity called "enjoyment." This is the good, well-ordered love that one has for things that are valuable in and of themselves. Augustine likes to use the metaphor of home to capture the feeling of enjoyment. Home is the place that you want to go for its own sake. You go to the bank or to the market for the sake of doing or getting something; you go home, in contrast, just to be. You can rest there. You experience a sense of comfort and peace. Your love for your home is the love of enjoyment.

Second, there is the charity called "use." Use is a good, well-ordered love that you have for things that are not valuable in themselves. For example, in order to make your home livable you need certain things from the bank and from the market. If your home is good in and of itself, and it depends on these other things, then they must be goods too. They are not, however, goods to be enjoyed. Suppose someone who is making a long journey home runs into various banks and markets along the way and is so distracted by them that she has no time at the end to enjoy her home. Surely this would be a terrible mismanagement of priorities. This person has tried to enjoy things that she should only have used. Your love for things that you need in order to love your home should be the love of use.

The mismanagement of use and enjoyment is what gives rise to cupidity. For Augustine, there are four possible psychological states:

1. Loving something as valuable in itself (enjoyment)
2. Loving something as not valuable in itself (use)
3. Enjoying something not valuable in itself (cupidity)
4. Using something valuable in itself (cupidity)

The first two states are right and good; the second two are wrong—human beings never ultimately succeed in these wrongful loves.

The trick in life is always to make sure that the nature of your love matches the nature of its object. This is what human beings are especially bad at—why we constantly find only misery. Although proper

love is impossible for human beings to put into practice, it is not difficult to understand. Augustine lays out his theory with breathtaking
simplicity:

The only thing that falls under category (1) is God. This is because
God is the only eternal good. Despite the illustration using markets,
banks and houses, according to Augustine, God is our only true home.

The entire rest of the universe falls under category (2). All crea-
tures, including family, friends, and even one's own mind and body are
only valuable in so far as they lead to God.

When human beings treat anything that is not God as valuable in
itself, we commit the sin of cupidity. If we treat God as a means to
achieving something else, we also commit cupidity. These two sides of
cupidity often go together. When a person prays that she will win the
lottery or find a boyfriend she proves (a) that she values things that are
not valuable and (b) that she is willing to use God to get them.

In a later work called *On Christian Teaching*, Augustine insists
that respecting the distinction between use and enjoyment is essential to
our happiness. He writes,

> So in this mortal life we are like travelers away from our Lord: if
> we wish to return to the homeland where we can be happy we must
> use this world, not enjoy it, in order to discern 'the invisible attrib-
> utes of God, which are understood through what has been made'
> or, in other words, to ascertain what is eternal and spiritual from
> corporeal and temporal things. [E 17]

Augustine presents his thesis as a straightforward application of Christian principles.

What Augustine's readers find so shocking about his thesis is the
claim that human beings are not valuable in themselves, that they are to
be used as mere instruments for the sake of something else. Does
Augustine really say this? Yes. He writes,

> Among all these things, then it is only the eternal unchangeable
> things which I mentioned that are to be enjoyed; other things are to
> be used so that we may attain the full enjoyment of those things.
> We ourselves who enjoy and use other things are things. . . . So if
> you ought to love yourself not on your own account but on account
> of the one who is the most proper object of your love, another per-
> son should not be angry if you love him too on account of God.
> For the divinely established rule of love says 'you shall love your
> neighbor as yourself' but God 'with all your heart, and with all
> your soul, and with all your mind,' so that you may devote all your
> thoughts and all your life and all your understanding to the one

from whom you actually receive the things that you devote to him.
[E 31]

It is Augustine's carefully considered opinion that when human beings rightly love each other they use each other to reach God.

Some of Augustine's readers balk at this view. They want to regard *On Christian Teaching* as anomalous or overstated. They cite other works in which Augustine seems to indicate that we should enjoy other human beings. Two things must be kept in mind, however.

First of all, *On Christian Teaching*, is not a minor work, but was widely read and highly influential throughout the Middle Ages. It was intended and used as a kind of manual for the training of priests. Hence, even if moderns prefer to disregard it, its historical importance cannot be ignored.

Second, Augustine recognizes and values logical consistency. He cannot consistently extend enjoyment to human beings. If human beings are fragile and if it is wrong to enjoy fragile things, then it is wrong to enjoy human beings. The only way for Augustine to deny that it is wrong to enjoy human beings would be for him to deny either that human beings are fragile or that it is wrong to enjoy fragile things.

He cannot deny the first without repudiating Christianity itself. The whole reason human beings need a savior is because they are fragile.

He cannot deny the second without repudiating his own theodicy. According to Augustine's theodicy, whatever causes suffering is evil. Enjoying fragile things necessarily causes suffering. Therefore, it must be evil. This logic goes to the very heart of Augustine's entire lifework. He is not about to give it up.

5.4 Voluntarism

Although Augustine's views on love may seem stark, they led to the development of an important tradition in ethics called voluntarism. The word "voluntarism" comes from the word "*voluntas*," which means "will" in Latin. Ethical voluntarism is best understood in contrast against ethical rationalism.

Ethical rationalists claim that reason is the proper source and guide for moral action. Classic examples of ethical rationalists are Socrates and Thomas Aquinas, both of whom maintained that, when human beings truly understand what they are doing, they never commit evil.

Ethical voluntarists, in contrast, claim that the will is the proper source and guide for moral action. Augustine maintains that even when human beings understand exactly what they are doing, they still commit evil. He uses his own experience as an example: recall the episode of the theft of pears, with which we began this book. Augustine knew this theft was wrong and pointless, and that is precisely why he did it. The episode proved to Augustine that ethics is more a matter for the heart than for the head.

Augustine defines virtue, not in terms of rationality, but in terms of "rightly ordered loves." [See *City of God* XV, 22.] In his view, as long as you love rightly, you can do no wrong. He encapsulates this idea in a catchphrase that appears in his sermons: "*Dilige et quod vis fac*" ("Love, and do what you will").

Augustine sets precedent for subsequent voluntarists by casting the will as the determining factor in human affairs. He writes,

> A body tends by its weight towards the place proper to it—weight does not necessarily tend towards the lowest place but towards its proper place. Fire tends upwards, stone downwards. By their weight they are moved and seek their proper place . . . My love is my weight: wherever I go my love is what brings me there. [D 265-6]

This point would later be championed by the Scottish philosopher David Hume (1711-76), whose entire ethical theory is based on the thesis that reason is the slave of the passions.

Nor does Augustine's conception of will find expression only among subsequent voluntarists. Immanuel Kant is an ethical rationalist, whose ethical theory is still important and popular today. Although Kant maintains that reason is the proper source and guide for moral action, he reserves a special role for the will within his theory. He famously asserts, "Nothing can possibly be conceived in the world, or even out of it, which can be called good without qualification, except a *good will*." [O 11] Although Kant is often credited with introducing this idea for the first time, he may well have lifted it straight out of the writings of the father of voluntarism. Augustine writes,

> To have a good will is to have something far more valuable than all earthly kingdoms and pleasures; to lack it is to lack something that only the will itself can give, something that is better than all the goods that are not in our power. [H 19-20]

The idea of "good will toward men" has become part of the very fabric of Western society.

Augustine's analysis of charity, cupidity, use, and enjoyment should make it clear that his voluntarism will always be couched within a strongly theological framework. For Augustine, good will is ultimately nothing other than the love of God. This is why Augustine is a

69

divine command theorist. He holds that an act is right if and only if it is done out of an intention to serve and obey the eternal God.

5.5 Against Culture and Education

Augustine's ethics carries direct political implications. The vast majority of political undertakings are designed to glorify and enjoy this fragile and temporary world in some way. Hence, for Augustine, the vast majority of political undertakings are wrong and doomed to failure. It does not matter whether Christians or pagans are running Rome. Anyone who invests in Rome is investing in the City of Man.

The alleged greatness of the Roman Empire lay in the sophistication of its culture. Theatre, architecture, sculpture, literature, mathematics, new technologies, etc. All of these accomplishments are largely due to the classical education that was widely available and encouraged for hundreds of years.

Somewhere between Socrates and Seneca (4 B.C.-65 A.D.), the concept of a liberal arts education was invented. Traditionally, the liberally educated person studied the *trivium* of grammar, rhetoric, and logic, and the *quadrivium* of arithmetic, geometry, music, and astronomy. The study of these arts would make you a free person. Philosophers of this period extolled the virtues of the educated man and praised the accomplishments in the arts and the sciences that it made possible. The Romans wanted, and in many cases succeeded, in making their world into a great cultural arena.

Augustine's invective against the City of Man, however, implies an invective against the culture and education that makes it possible. An important part of *City of God* is devoted precisely to this task. Augustine argues that culture and education are not the great and noble things they appear to be.

Augustine was living during the final dissolution the golden age of classical learning. He stood on the threshold of the period of Western history that would later be known as the Dark Ages, due to its widespread anti-intellectualism. The truth is that Augustine did his part to encourage this trend.

It may seem strange that a man who himself received a classical education and gained his power as bishop because of it, would argue against it. This is like a man who climbs a ladder and exclaims at the view from the roof as tears the ladder to pieces on the grounds that ladders are evil.

Augustine's position will not seem so strange, however, upon closer consideration of his experience with education. Augustine tells us in the *Confessions* that he found studying tiresome. The only thing that kept him going was the belief that it would somehow enable him to transcend the miseries of this world.

At first, he thought of this transcendence in purely material terms: education would land him a good job with income enough to make the misery go away. He was bitterly disappointed on this score.

Then, during his neoplatonic days, Augustine began to think of the promised transcendence in more mystical terms. Neoplatonists believed that contemplation of the truth would lead to an ecstatic vision that would make the misery go away. He was bitterly disappointed on this score as well.

Augustine decided that the only thing that made the misery go away was believing in God. He also decided that one does not need any cultural refinement to achieve this. It is not at all surprising, therefore, to find Augustine promoting philistinism.

In *On Christian Teaching*, Augustine argues against the main pillars of liberal arts education. Concerning science, he writes,

> In itself, this knowledge, although not implicating one in superstition, does not give much help—almost none, in fact—in interpreting the divine scripture and is really more of a hindrance, since it demands the fruitless expenditure of effort. Because it is akin to the deadly error of those who prophesy fatuously about fate, it is more convenient and honorable to despise it. [E 111]

Views like this were not unusual in the ancient world and can be found in neoplatonic authors such as Claudius Ptolemy (c.100-c.178). In his *Almagest*, Ptolemy sets out the geocentric astronomical system that dominated Western astronomy into the seventeenth century. In his introductory remarks, Ptolemy argues that the science of earthly things is a waste of time because they are always in a state of flux and corruption. Augustine would agree with this. What he would not agree with is Ptolemy's claim that, in studying the celestial movements, one is studying more eternal and perfect objects, and hence gaining insight into the nature of things divine.

Concerning the arts, Augustine writes,

> In human life knowledge of these things is to be used sparingly and in passing, and not in order to make things—unless a particular task demands it, which is not my concern now—but to assist our judgement, so that we are not entirely unaware of what scripture wishes to convey when it includes figurative expressions based on these arts. [E 111]

He summarizes his findings:

> So it seems to me that the following advice is beneficial for young people who are keen and intelligent, who fear God and seek a life of true happiness. Do not venture without due care into any branches of learning which are pursued outside the church of Christ, as if they were a means to attaining the happy life, but discriminate sensibly and carefully between them. [E 122-3]

Augustine does not deny that there may be some useful things in classical learning. But he warns that any such things "must be removed by Christians and applied to their true function, that of preaching the gospel." [E 125]

One might suspect from this last comment that Augustine is in favor of replacing the secular culture of the City of Man with a Christian alternative. Why not set up Christian schools to teach Christian subjects and propagate Christian activities for the public to enjoy?

Augustine does not make this move, however, for two reasons. First of all, the proliferation of false conversion would make any allowance of culture dangerous in his view. Secondly, in his analysis, combining culture and religion is the very mistake that the Romans made. Augustine admires the religious devotion of the early Empire. By making their religion a public affair, however, they denigrated it to the point of sacrilege. The pornographic theater shows were a case in point. Augustine writes,

> When I was a young man I used to go to sacrilegious shows and entertainments. I watched the antics of madmen; I listened to singing boys; I thoroughly enjoyed the most degrading spectacles put on in the honor of gods and goddesses—in honor of the Heavenly Virgin, and of Berecynthia, mother of all. On the yearly festival of Berecynthia's purification the lowest kind of actors sang, in front of her litter, songs unfit for the ears of even the mother of one of those mountebanks to say nothing of the mother of any decent citizen. [C 51]

Augustine was convinced that attempts at Christian culture, such as the Festival of the Martyrs, were of the same genre. If theaters are an excuse for prostitution and public celebration in general is a form of idolatry, we should not encourage them.

Augustine longs for a simple society composed only of the Church and the family. It would be devoid not only of education, arts, and sciences, but government as well. The function of the government is to regulate culture. Without culture, there would be no need for it. Given however, that culture springs up like a mushroom wherever human beings can be found, government cannot be avoided. Augustine's final word on the matter is that politics is a necessary evil.

5.6 Augustine's Political Pessimism

Philosophers commonly assert that politics is a necessary evil. For most of them, however, this is an overstatement. Most of them, like Plato and Aristotle, believe that government has some positive role to play in human lives. Being political optimists, they think of the state as having legitimate or just authority. Their theories are driven by this question: *What is the source and extent of just political authority?* The question assumes that there is justification for the state.

Augustine does not make this assumption. The central question driving his political philosophy is more basic. Augustine asks, *Is there any just political authority?* And his answer is a resounding *no*. So for him, the other question, the question that occupied so many of his ancient predecessors and modern successors, is moot. This is what confirms Augustine's place as a rockbottom political pessimist in the history of political thought.

There have been other political pessimists in the history of political thought, of course. Many of them, however, use their denunciation of the state as justification for libertarian ideals or as impetus for anarchy. If the state's authority is unjust, then it must be overthrown! Human beings should strive to achieve an apolitical utopia instead.

Once again, Augustine sets himself apart. In book XIX of *City of God,* Augustine tackles the question of the justice of political authority. He defends the paradoxical position that all political authority is unjust *and yet must be obeyed.*

Although this position is paradoxical, unusual among philosophers and perhaps original with Augustine, it is not at all rare in Christian thinking. In fact, it becomes such a central theme in Christian thought that later Christian philosophers like Thomas Aquinas and John Locke (1632-1704) have to bend over backwards to invent political theories that are both Christian and optimistic at the same time. Jean-Jacques Rousseau (1712-78) despairs of this possibility. He concludes that Christians will always be slaves because they do not care enough about this world.

Augustine would unhesitatingly accept this charge. But why? Why does he think that unjust political authority must be obeyed? In order to answer this question we first must understand exactly why Augustine thought all political authority is unjust.

5.7 Justice

Augustine defines justice as "that virtue which gives to each his due." [C 882] In his view, to say that political authority is unjust is to say that it does not give to each his due. Political authority necessarily orders human beings in an unfitting manner. As Augustine often puts it, it is perverse.

The great chain of being provides a basis for understanding Augustine's distinction between just and unjust order. God created a variety of beings in the universe, each with its own level of existence. Since existence is equivalent to goodness, these things can be ranked on a scale. Angels are superior to human beings, and human beings are superior to horses. The reason is that each species of creature is made from a portion of the form of the good, and each portion of the form of the good contains a different amount of goodness. Angels all share the angelic form, which contains a lot of goodness; human beings all share the human form, which contains less goodness; and horses all share the horse form, which contains still less goodness. This is the natural order among things.

Justice comes from treating each thing in accordance with its position in the natural order. Augustine makes an assumption about proper treatment, which we will call the principle of authority:

Principle of Authority: x has the right to command y if and only if x is superior to y.

Human beings are superior to horses. Therefore, we have the right to command them. Angels are superior to human beings. Therefore, they have the right to command us. Finally, since God is superior to everybody, he has the right to command us all.

Political authority is perverse because it defies the principle of authority. Human beings are all equally good on the great chain of being. Therefore, none has the right to command another. Yet the state gives some human beings command over others. Thus, the state does not give to each his due. Augustine writes, "Remove justice and what are kingdoms but gangs of criminals on a large scale?" [C 139]

One might think it would be easy to use the great chain of being to justify hierarchy among human beings. All one would need to claim is that some human beings have more of the form of the good in them than others. No doubt there have been many rulers through the ages who have believed that they and their line are naturally superior to the rest of humanity.

74

This view, however, presents a deep philosophical difficulty. Human beings are all members of the same kind precisely because we were all made from the same portion of the form of the good. The same portion of the form of the good necessarily has the same amount of goodness in it. How, therefore, can one human being be superior to another? Either those with political authority are made from the human form, in which case they are naturally equivalent to all other humans, or they are made from a different form, in which case, they are not humans. One might try to finesse a response here, but very few philosophers are willing to go so far as to say that those with political authority are literally superhuman.

Of course, there are plenty of other ways to argue that political authority is just. One might even argue for hierarchy among human beings on the basis of some acquired characteristic such as virtue or divine anointment. The point is that, given Augustine's commitments, it is not surprising to find him ignoring these possibilities. Augustine's argument can be summarized as follows:

1. Justice requires giving each his due.
2. Giving each his due is treating each in accordance with his place in the natural order.
3. Human beings are equal on the natural order.
4. Therefore, justice requires treating human beings as equals.
5. The state does not treat human beings as equals.
6. Therefore, the state is unjust.

Although this argument is controversial every step of the way, its logical form is irreproachable.

As always, Augustine finds support for his neoplatonic approach in the Bible. He writes,

> This relationship is prescribed by the order of nature, and it is in this situation that God created man. For he says "Let him have lordship over the fish of the sea, the birds of the sky . . . and all the reptiles that crawl on the earth." He did not wish the rational being, made in his own image, to have dominion over any but irrational creatures, not man over man, but man over the beasts. [C 874]

To have dominion over something is to have rightful command over it.

Augustine's principle of authority is perhaps the most tenuous link in his argument. It bears a certain resemblance to the neoplatonic causal principle, which we have seen Augustine use on a number of occasions. The causal principle states that if x is superior to y, then x has causal power over y. This is supposed to follow from the fact that a superior being has more existence than its inferior. Yet, even supposing that we have proved that *x* has causal power over *y*, this is still a far cry from proving that it has *rightful command* over *y*. Augustine leaps from the concept of causal power to the concept of rightful command without explanation. Perhaps the only explanation is that this is the way God commands it to be.

Another thing that complicates Augustine's theory is the fact that he seems in some places to treat women as naturally inferior to men. He occasionally makes disparaging comments about women. For example, in *The Literal Meaning of Genesis* he writes,

> The woman then, with the appearance and distinctive physical characteristics of her sex, was made for the man from the man. . . .
> Consequently, when someone asks what help the woman was intended to give the man, as I carefully consider to the best of my ability all that we are told, I can think of no other purpose than the procreation of children in order to fill the earth with their descendants. [I, II, 82]

Augustine is clearly sexist, just as one would expect a fourth century Roman citizen to be.

Augustine's sexism, however, need not imply that he places men higher on the great chain of being than women. On the same page as the above quoted passage, Augustine says that it is right for husbands to command wives, and for parents to command children. Nevertheless, he adds that in a good family, the husband's commands are commands of care rather than commands of domination. Augustine gives men the role of issuing commands of care, not because he sees men as naturally superior, but because he sees them as better suited to that role. He views women and children much the way he might view a man lacking a limb. Such beings are not essentially different, and therefore not inferior; they are just accidentally different, and therefore suited to a different role than a man with all of his limbs. This differential treatment is still objectionable, but it is not enough to undermine the consistency of his theory.

Setting these difficulties aside, we are now in a position to see why all political authority is unjust. Political authority is the command of domination, and it is unjust for equals to dominate one another. If this is so, however, then why must political authority be obeyed? Why not resist and banish politics instead?

5.8 The State as Penal Order

Augustine enthusiastically affirms that in heaven all politics will be banished, and that human beings should try to use the heavenly city as a model for this world wherever political authority falls short. At the same time, however, he maintains that we have no right to resist political authority where we find it. The reason is that political authority constitutes suffering and suffering constitutes our punishment for original sin. God would not allow human beings to suffer without a reason. Therefore, he would not allow political authority to exist without a reason. To defy political authority is to defy God.

Political authority constitutes suffering both for those who do the dominating and for those who are dominated. The reason is that both are enslaved. The dominated are enslaved to their dominators and their dominators are enslaved to sin. Augustine writes,

> Now, as our Lord above says, "Everyone who commits sin is sin's slave," and that is why, though many devout men are slaves to un-righteous masters, yet the masters they serve are not themselves free men; "for when a man is conquered by another he is also bound as a slave to his conqueror." And obviously it is a happier lot to be slave to a human being that to a lust; and, in fact, the most pitiless domination that devastates the hearts of men, is that exercised by this very lust for domination, to mention no others. [C 785]

According to Augustine, human beings cannot help enjoying dominating one another. Political authority gives rise to the lust for domination and this lust is the epitome of cupidity.

Although political authority is illegitimate, it must be obeyed because God is using it as his way of punishing us. Political authority is never just on the political level as political authority, but it is just on the cosmic level as an apt form of punishment. Augustine asks, "If God's reasons are inscrutable, does that mean that they are unjust?" [C 216] Our perverse wills merit perverse treatment. This is to say that the state constitutes a penal order. Augustine uses a strange and interesting analogy to describe the situation. [See C 869f.]

Suppose you are hanging upside down. Both legs are bound together by a rope and the rope is suspended from a tree limb. This position is uncomfortable and unnatural to you. Even if you are blindfolded, you can tell in your very loins that something is wrong, and you have a general idea of what you would need to do to feel better. But you cannot do it. You would need someone else to cut the rope.

Now suppose further that you are required to hold a heavy stone in each hand. This makes your position even more uncomfortable. Your arms grow fatigued with the weight. You would be very grateful if someone would come along and hold the stones for you. Then you could let your arms dangle. After holding the stones for some amount time, being allowed to let your arms dangle will be a welcome relief. You may even feel positively comfortable for a moment. Before long, though, you will realize that you are still upside down.

This analogy is meant to illustrate the situation of the human race. Ever since the sin of Adam and Eve, human beings have had misdirected wills. This is an extremely uncomfortable position. The only remedy for it is for God to put us right again. In good time, he will put some of us right through grace. Meanwhile, maintaining some degree of order in this world constitutes an extra burden for us. Politicians come along and offer to do this for us. It feels to us as a relief. But it is not a salvation. Augustine writes,

> Thus they have amongst them some tranquillity of order, and therefore some peace. But they are still wretched just because, although they enjoy some degree of serenity and freedom from suffering, they are not in a condition where they have the right to be serene and free from pain. They are yet more wretched, however, if they are not at peace with the law by which the natural order is governed. [C 871]

The unhappy truth seems to be that human beings need to be at peace with their punishment for original sin, and accept the terrible relief that political authority provides.

Despite his knowledge of the evil of politics, Augustine also left some space in his life for idealism. He founded what is considered to be the first religious order in the West. Before he was bishop, he and a group of male friends set up a household devoted to the study and worship of God. After he became bishop, he established what has since come to be known as the Augustinian Order. According to the rules of this order, members are required to renounce all property rights. They do not even own the clothing on their backs. In banishing ownership, Augustine hoped to banish domination. His goal was to establish a small pocket of society as free from politics as possible.

Augustine would have far rather retired from politics altogether. Nevertheless, he accepted his share of the burden. He tried to live what he called "the mixed life": enough involvement to remember the plight of humanity; enough leisure to remember the promise of God.

6

Augustine's Legacy

Augustine's extraordinary influence on the history of Western thought is often explained in virtue of his dominance during the Middle Ages. Of course, literacy plummeted in Europe in the centuries following Augustine's death. Due to the shortage of writing materials and the shortage of readers, not many books circulated. Nevertheless, it has been estimated that, for almost a thousand years, Augustine's texts circulated more than any other single set of texts next to the Bible. Until the twelfth century, only a handful of other philosophy books were available for those few who had the ability and the leisure to read them. Even granting this, we can still ask why Augustine so dominated the Middle Ages.

Some would say that he was lucky: his writing happened to survive during a very sterile period, and, because there was not much else to choose from, his thought became ubiquitous. Others would say that Augustine's writing survived and prevailed precisely because it was so rich and well rounded. Perhaps the truth lies somewhere in between.

Naturally, Augustine's dominance seems much more of a mystery to anyone who has the luxury to stand on his shoulders. At least two further factors, however, make Augustine's thought difficult for contemporary readers to appreciate. First, Augustine regards the search as more important than the discovery. This makes his work seem inconclusive and rambling. Second, Augustine regards philosophy as the handmaiden of religious belief, not the queen of the sciences. This makes his work seem short on rigor and long on rhetoric. Because of these two factors, Augustine's achievement was much more accessible to the pre-modern mind.

Although Augustine primarily represents the preoccupations of the Middle Ages, the Middle Ages comprise a vast portion of the history of Western thought. Medieval philosophy did not evolve into modern philosophy until the seventeenth century, and even then, many philosophers and other intellectuals were still using medieval sources. Hence, it is in virtue of Augustine's dominance in the Middle Ages as well as the dominance of the Middle Ages itself that Augustine became such an extraordinary influence on the history of Western thought.

In this book, we have surveyed the highlights of his contribution. We encountered prototypes of St. Anselm's ontological argument, René Descartes' *Cogito*, the notion of a crucial experiment that would have been recognizable to Sir Francis Bacon or Sir Karl Popper, and a theory of time very much like the one advanced by Edmund Husserl. We saw a sophisticated innatist theory of language and knowledge, as well as hints at the existence of a subconscious that would lie dormant in Western thought for fifteen hundred years. In Augustine's theodicy, we witnessed an almost Calvinist conception of salvation through grace, two classic solutions to the problem of evil, and, most importantly, the first robust philosophical account of the notion of a will. In *City of God*, we discovered the roots of voluntarism and the foundation of monasticism. Finally, in *Confessions*, we found the first extensive use of autobiography to provide inspiration for those who seek the truth about themselves and the world. All things considered, it is hard not to be impressed with the scope of this contribution.

Perhaps Augustine was lucky as to have lived when he did so that his works would have such a profound influence. If so, it was lucky for us.

Bibliography

All of Augustine's works were originally written in Latin. Almost all of them have been edited, and almost all of them have been translated, often several times. Throughout this book, we used quotations from the best of the existing translations. The letter codes we use in citations refer to the list of works below. Roman numerals after the letter indicate volume numbers, if any. Arabic numerals indicate page numbers.

Works Cited:

[A] Augustine, *Against the Academics and The Teacher*, Peter King, tr., Indianapolis: Hackett, 1995.

[B] —————, *The Catholic and Manichaean Ways of Life*, Donald A. Gallagher and Idella J. Gallagher, trs., Washington: The Catholic University Press, 1966.

[C] —————, *City of God*, Henry Bettenson, tr., Middlesex: Penguin, 1984.

[D] —————, *Confessions*, F. J. Sheed, tr., Indianapolis: Hackett, 1993.

[E] —————, *De Doctrina Christiana*, R. P. H. Green, tr., Oxford: Clarendon, 1995.

[F] —————, *Earlier Writings*, John H. S. Burleigh, tr., Philadelphia: Westminister Press, 1953.

[G] —————, *Eighty-three Different Questions*, David L. Mosher, tr., Washington: Catholic University Press, 1982.

[H] —————, *On Free Choice of the Will*, Thomas Williams, tr., Indianapolis: Hackett, 1993.

[I] —————, *The Literal Meaning of Genesis*, vols. I-II, John Hammond Taylor, tr., New York: Newman Press, 1982.

[J] —————, *St. Augustine's De Musica: A Synopsis*, W. F. Jackson Knight, tr., London: The Orthological Institute, 1949.

[K] —————, *The Works of Saint Augustine: A Translation for the 21st Century*, John E. Rotelle, ed., New York: New City Press, 1990-.

[L] —————, *(Writings of) Saint Augustine*, vols. I-LX, Ludwig Schopp, *et al.*, ed., *Fathers of the Church: A New Translation*, New York: Cima and Fathers of the Church, Inc., and Washington D.C.: Catholic University Press of America, 1947-68.

[M] Brann, Eva, *What, Then, is Time?*, Oxford: Roman and Littlefield, 1999.

[N] Descartes, René, *Discourse on Method and Meditations on First Philosophy*, Donald A. Cress, tr., Indianapolis: Hackett, 1980.

[O] Kant, Immanuel, *Fundamental Principles of the Metaphysic of Morals*, Thomas K. Abbot, tr., Indianapolis: Bobbs-Merrill, 1949.

For Further Reference:

Adams, Marilyn McCord and Robert Merrihew Adams, eds., *The Problem of evil*, Oxford: Oxford University Press, 1990.

Augustine, *The Essential Augustine*, Vernon J. Bourke, ed., Indianapolis: Hackett, 1974.

Brown, Peter, *Augustine of Hippo, A Biography*, London: Fabor and Faber, 1990.

Chadwick, Henry, *Augustine,* Oxford: Oxford University Press, 1986.

Gale, Richard (ed.), *The Philosophy of Time,* London: MacMillan, 1968.

Kirwan, Christopher, *Augustine,* New York: Routledge, 1989.

Gilson, Etienne, *The Christian Philosophy of St. Augustine,* New York: Random House, 1960.

O'Connell, Robert J., *St. Augustine's Early Theory of Man, A.D. 386-391,* Cambridge: Harvard University Press, 1968.

O'Daly, Gerard, *Augustine's Philosophy of Mind,* Berkeley: University of California Press, 1987.

Plantinga, Alvin, *The Ontological Argument: From St. Anselm to Contemporary Philosophers,* Garden City: Anchor Books, 1965.

Wittgenstein, Ludwig, *The Blue and Brown Books,* New York: Harper and Row, 1965.

—————, *Philosophical Investigations,* G. E. M. Anscombe, tr., New York: MacMillan, 1968.